JUNIOR READING EXPERT

A Theme-Based Reading Course for Young EFL Learners

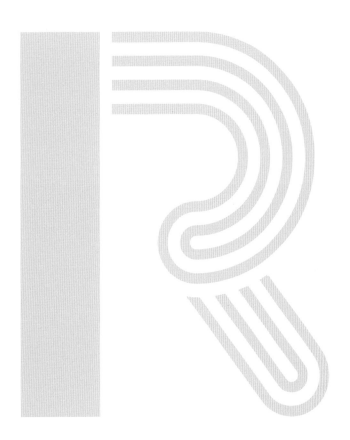

Level **1**

JUNIOR
READING EXPERT

Level 1

Series Editor	Ji-hyun Kim
Project Editors	Eun-kyung Kim, Jun-hee Kim, Yoon-joung Choi
Contributing Writers	Curtis Thompson, Bryce Olk, Angela Hai Yue Lan, Patrick Ferraro, MyAn Le, Keeran Murphy
Illustrators	Soo-hyeon Lee, Mi-rae Shin, Sun-kyung Ha, Seol-hui Kim
Design	Hoon-jung Ahn, Ji-young Ki
Editorial Designer	Sun-hee Kim
ISBN	979-11-253-4040-9 53740
Photo Credits	www.shutterstock.com

3rd Edition
Copyright © 2023 NE Neungyule, Inc.
First Printing 5 January 2023
6th Printing 15 May 2024

INTRODUCTION

Junior Reading Expert is a four-level reading course for EFL readers, with special relevance for older elementary school students and junior high school students. Students will acquire not only reading skills but also knowledge of various contemporary and academic topics.

Features

Covers Dynamic, Contemporary Topics

Engaging topics, including culture, sports, and literature, are developed in an easy and interesting way to motivate students.

Expands Knowledge

Each unit is composed of two closely related readings under one topic heading. These readings allow students to explore the theme in depth.

Features Longer Passages

EFL students are seldom exposed to long reading passages and therefore tend to find them difficult. Compelling and well-developed passages designed specifically for EFL students will help them learn to handle longer passages with ease.

Presents Different Text Types of Passages

Reading passages are presented as articles, letters, debates, interviews, and novels. This helps students become familiarized with a variety of writing formats and styles through different genres of readings.

Provides Various Exercises for Reading Skills

All readings are accompanied by different types of tasks, such as multiple choice, matching, short answer, true/false, and fill-in-the-blank. These exercises are carefully designed to develop the following reading skills: understanding main ideas, identifying details, drawing inferences, and recognizing organizational structures.

Series Overview

Each level of *Junior Reading Expert* is composed of 20 units, with two related readings accompanying each unit. The number of words in each Reading 1 passage is as follows:

Level 1: 150–170 words
Level 2: 170–190 words
Level 3: 190–210 words
Level 4: 210–230 words

Format

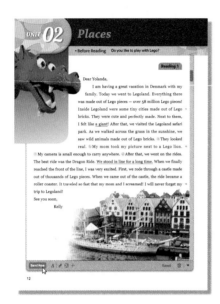

Reading 1

Reading 1 takes students into the first of the unit's two readings. Being the main reading of the unit, Reading 1 deals with various interesting and important topics in great depth. The passages gradually increase in difficulty as students progress through the book.

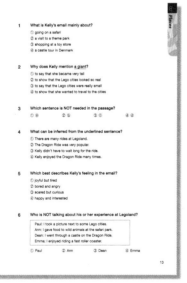

Different Types of Questions

A full page of different types of questions follows Reading 1. The questions concentrate on important reading skills, such as understanding the main idea, identifying details, drawing inferences, and recognizing the organizational structure.

Reading 2

Reading 2 offers a second reading passage on the unit topic, the length of which is from 90 to 110 words. Reading 2 supplements Reading 1 with additional information, further explanation, or a new point of view.

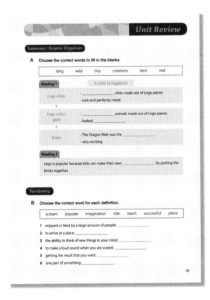

Unit Review

A Summary / Graphic Organizer
Either a summary or a graphic organizer is provided for Reading 1 and Reading 2 to facilitate a better understanding of the flow of passages. Performing this task also encourages the development of systematic comprehension skills.

B Vocabulary
Each unit is concluded with vocabulary practice. It checks students' knowledge of essential vocabulary words. Vocabulary practice requires students to either match definitions or choose words in context.

Table of Contents

Unit 01 **Food**
Reading 1   Marshmallows   8
Reading 2   The Whoopie Pie   10

Unit 02 **Places**
Reading 1   Legoland   12
Reading 2   The Lego Company   14

Unit 03 **Jobs**
Reading 1   Graffiti Artist   16
Reading 2   At the Center of Graffiti   18

Unit 04 **Animals**
Reading 1   Prairie Dogs   20
Reading 2   Prairie Dogs' Burrows   22

Unit 05 **Entertainment**
Reading 1   *The Lion King*   24
Reading 2   Julie Taymor   26

Unit 06 **Psychology**
Reading 1   The Zeigarnik Effect   28
Reading 2   The Self-Reference Effect   30

Unit 07 **Science**
Reading 1   Bad Breath   32
Reading 2   Bad Morning Breath   34

Unit 08 **Sports**
Reading 1   Golf   36
Reading 2   Golf Balls   38

Unit 09 **Society**
Reading 1   Habitat for Humanity   40
Reading 2   Volunteer Vacations   42

Unit 10 **Literature**
Reading 1   An Extract From *Anne of Green Gables*   44
Reading 2   Lucy Maud Montgomery   46

Unit 11	*Culture*	Reading 1	Kiwis in New Zealand	48
		Reading 2	The Maori	50
Unit 12	*Issues*	Reading 1	Vegan Diets	52
		Reading 2	Meat-Like Foods	54
Unit 13	*History*	Reading 1	Lincoln's Beard	56
		Reading 2	Honest Abe	58
Unit 14	*The Economy*	Reading 1	Why Coins Are Round	60
		Reading 2	Benefits of Using Cash	62
Unit 15	*Festivals*	Reading 1	The Albuquerque International Balloon Fiesta	64
		Reading 2	Ride a Balloon in Cappadocia	66
Unit 16	*The Environment*	Reading 1	Earth Hour	68
		Reading 2	WWF	70
Unit 17	*Space*	Reading 1	Created by Space Research	72
		Reading 2	Is Space Research Necessary?	74
Unit 18	*Technology*	Reading 1	Geothermal Energy	76
		Reading 2	A Solar-Powered Device	78
Unit 19	*The Arts*	Reading 1	Transporting Art	80
		Reading 2	No Flash at Museums	82
Unit 20	*People*	Reading 1	Harriet Tubman	84
		Reading 2	Harriet Tubman on the $20 Bill	86

Food

Reading 1

Marshmallows are a soft and tasty snack. They are used in puddings, chocolate bars, and many other desserts. But what does "marshmallow" mean? The word "marshmallow" comes from a plant's ____(A)____ and the ____(B)____ it grows. This plant is called a wild 5 *mallow. It grows in wetlands called marshes.

Long ago, Greeks used marshmallows to heal injuries. They were like medicine! Later, Egyptians made a dessert with them. They mixed them with nuts and honey. But modern marshmallows came from France. In the nineteenth 10 century, French candy store owners mixed mallow plant roots with sugar, egg whites, and water. People loved them! But they took too long to make, so gelatin was used instead of the mallow plant. For this reason, today's marshmallows don't have any mallow plant in them.

Nowadays, people love to make s'mores with marshmallows. To make one, you 15 roast a marshmallow and put it on a cracker with chocolate. The name means "gimme some more." And after you try one, you'll want more too!

*mallow: a type of plant that has pink, purple, or white flowers

1 **What is the best title for the passage?**

① What Is in the Marshmallow?

② The Origin of a Soft, Tasty Snack

③ Marshmallow as a Healing Medicine

④ How a Greek Dessert Spread around the World

2 **What is the best pair for blanks (A) and (B)?**

① size — season

② name — place

③ color — way

④ shape — reason

3 **In France, why was gelatin used to make marshmallows instead of the mallow plant?**

① to get rid of dangerous things

② to make marshmallows softer

③ to reduce the price of marshmallows

④ to produce more marshmallows at a time

4 **It can be inferred from the 2nd paragraph that** _____.

① marshmallows were created by accident

② marshmallows cannot be made without nuts

③ marshmallows were not used as food in the past

④ marshmallows have changed little by little over time

5 **What is NOT true about marshmallows?**

① They are added in many kinds of desserts.

② They were used as a medicine in Greece.

③ Egyptians ate them with nuts and honey.

④ A French cook made the marshmallows of today.

6 **In order to make a s'more, roast a marshmallow and** _____

_____.

The whoopie pie is a traditional American dessert. It is made of two cake-like cookies with a cream center. This cream is usually vanilla flavored, and chocolate cookies are typically used. However, pumpkin and gingerbread cookies can be used too. Whoopie pies are certainly a 5 delicious treat. But where did their unusual name come from? According to one legend, excited children would yell "Whoopee!" when they received one. People have been enjoying whoopie pies for many years, and they are still popular today. In fact, in 2011, the whoopie pie even became the official state treat of the US state of Maine. 10

What is the best title for the passage?

① A Beloved American Treat

② The Best Way to Enjoy Pies

③ Whoopee: How This Fun Word Was Made

④ The Cookie: From a Snack to a National Treat

⑤ The Secret Recipe for a Delicious Whoopie Pie

Summary / Graphic Organizer

A Choose the correct words to fill in the blanks.

| roots | dessert | delicious | modern | wetlands | injury |

Reading 1

Marshmallow ▶ marsh: _____ + mallow: a wild plant's name

| Greece | Marshmallows were used as medicine. |

| Egypt | Mixed with nuts and honey, marshmallows were made into a(n) _____. |

| France | - Candy store owners used sugar, egg whites, and water with mallow plant _____.
- Later, gelatin was used instead of the mallow plant, like in _____ marshmallows. |

Reading 2

The whoopie pie has been enjoyed as a(n) _____ treat for years across America.

Vocabulary

B Choose the correct word for each definition.

| legend | unusual | owner | tasty | heal | spread | medicine |

1 having a good flavor: _____

2 to become or make well again: _____

3 not happening very often; not commonly seen or heard: _____

4 a story about past people and events that may or may not be true: _____

5 to affect or cover more and more of something: _____

6 something you take to cure sickness: _____

• Before Reading   Do you like to play with Lego?

Reading 1

Dear Yolanda,

I am having a great vacation in Denmark with my family. Today we went to Legoland. Everything there was made out of Lego pieces—over 58 million Lego pieces! Inside Legoland were some tiny cities made out of Lego ⁵ bricks. They were cute and perfectly made. Next to them, I felt like a giant! After that, we visited the Legoland safari park. As we walked across the grass in the sunshine, we saw wild animals made out of Lego bricks. ⓐThey looked real. ⓑMy mom took my picture next to a Lego lion. ¹⁰ ⓒMy camera is small enough to carry anywhere. ⓓAfter that, we went on the rides. The best ride was the Dragon Ride. We stood in line for a long time. When we finally reached the front of the line, I was very excited. First, we rode through a castle made out of thousands of Lego pieces. When we came out of the castle, the ride became a roller coaster. It traveled so fast that my mom and I screamed! I will never forget my ¹⁵ trip to Legoland!

See you soon,

　　Kelly

Send Now   _A_ 🔗 🖼 ＋   Saved 🗑 | ▼

1 **What is Kelly's email mainly about?**

① going on a safari

② a visit to a theme park

③ shopping at a toy store

④ a castle tour in Denmark

2 **Why does Kelly mention a giant?**

① to say that she became very tall

② to show that the Lego cities looked so real

③ to say that the Lego cities were really small

④ to show that she wanted to travel to the cities

3 **Which sentence is NOT needed in the passage?**

① ⓐ   ② ⓑ   ③ ⓒ   ④ ⓓ

4 **What can be inferred from the underlined sentence?**

① There are many rides at Legoland.

② The Dragon Ride was very popular.

③ Kelly didn't have to wait long for the ride.

④ Kelly enjoyed the Dragon Ride many times.

5 **Which best describes Kelly's feeling in the email?**

① joyful but tired

② bored and angry

③ scared but curious

④ happy and interested

6 **Who is NOT talking about his or her experience at Legoland?**

> Paul: I took a picture next to some Lego cities.
>
> Ann: I gave food to wild animals at the safari park.
>
> Dean: I went through a castle on the Dragon Ride.
>
> Emma: I enjoyed riding a fast roller coaster.

① Paul   ② Ann   ③ Dean   ④ Emma

The Lego brick is one of the most successful toys in history. In 2000, it was chosen as the "Toy of the Century." So why do children love Lego so much? Perhaps it is because _____. Children can put Lego pieces together to ⁵ make their own creations. The name Lego comes from the Danish words *leg godt*. They mean "play well." And in Latin, Lego means "I put together." Since they were created, more than 400 billion Lego pieces have been sold. That's more than 62 for every person in the world!

What is the best choice for the blank?

① their parents bought it for them

② they can enjoy the toys with friends

③ Lego lets them use their imagination

④ you can find Lego all around the world

⑤ Lego bricks are safe for them to play with

Summary / Graphic Organizer

A Choose the correct words to fill in the blanks.

long	wild	tiny	creations	best	real

Reading 1

A Visit to Legoland

Lego cities	- _____ cities made out of Lego pieces - cute and perfectly made

▼

Lego safari park	- _____ animals made out of Lego pieces - looked _____

▼

Rides	- The Dragon Ride was the _____. - very exciting

Reading 2

Lego is popular because kids can make their own _____ by putting the bricks together.

Vocabulary

B Choose the correct word for each definition.

scream	popular	imagination	ride	reach	successful	piece

1 enjoyed or liked by a large amount of people: _____

2 to arrive at a place: _____

3 the ability to think of new things in your mind: _____

4 to make a loud sound when you are scared: _____

5 getting the result that you want: _____

6 one part of something: _____

Reading 1

Do you love art? (ⓐ) I do. (ⓑ) I'm a graffiti artist in New York. (ⓒ) What's graffiti? (ⓓ) Usually, it's done outside on buildings or fences.

I use spray paint, markers, and stencils to draw graffiti. At first, I put my art in the neighborhood streets. But now I 5 work in my own studio! After I finish an artwork, I put my name on it. Some graffiti artists use their real name, but I use a fake one. I think it makes the art more interesting. Graffiti artists, like me, often teach themselves how to draw. Some people go to an art school, though. Because graffiti 10 is done in _____(A)_____, people used to think it was a social problem. But these days, it's seen as a form of modern art. You can even see it in art galleries!

Like other artists, graffiti artists use art to express their thoughts to the world. So, I'm always proud to show off my work.

1 **What is the passage mainly about?**

① the origin of graffiti

② what a graffiti artist does

③ how to teach yourself to draw

④ why some artists use a fake name

2 **Where would the following sentence best fit?**

It's art—paintings, drawings, and writing—on walls.

① ⓐ   ② ⓑ   ③ ⓒ   ④ ⓓ

3 **What is mentioned about the names graffiti artists use?**

① All graffiti artists should use fake names.

② A fake name can make the art more interesting.

③ Graffiti artists can use real names only in their neighborhood.

④ Graffiti artists put their name on their artwork before they paint it.

4 **What is the best choice for blank (A)?**

① New York

② art schools

③ public spaces

④ private spaces

5 **Write T if the statement is true and F if it's false.**

(1) The writer uses spray paint, fabric, and stencils to draw graffiti.

(2) Some graffiti artists study at an art school.

6 **Graffiti artists, as well as other artists,** _____

_____ **through art.**

At the Center of Graffiti

Come to see our new art show, *At the Center of Graffiti*! We're bringing art from the streets to our gallery walls. You can see over 100 pieces of art such as prints, photos, sculptures, and large works on entire walls. Join us to celebrate graffiti's growth into a popular modern art form!

General Information
- When: May - September 2024
- Where: Brooklyn Museum (100 Central Street, Brooklyn, NY)

TICKET PRICING

Adult	$22
Senior (Ages 65+)	$16
Student	$14
Child (Ages 4-12)	$10

OPENING HOURS

DAY	OPEN	CLOSE	LAST ENTRY
MON – WED	12:00 a.m.	7:00 p.m.	6:00 p.m.
THU – FRI	11:00 a.m.	8:00 p.m.	7:00 p.m.
WEEKEND	10:30 a.m.	8:30 p.m.	7:30 p.m.

Go to www.atthecenterofgraffiti.com for more information on this experience.

What is NOT true about the art show?

① There will be different types of artwork with graffiti.

② It is held for a total of five months.

③ Seniors pay less than students for their ticket.

④ The museum closes an hour after last entry.

⑤ The museum's hours are the longest on the weekend.

18

Summary / Graphic Organizer

A Choose the correct words to fill in the blanks.

interesting	public	galleries	express	finish

Reading 1

Graffiti is a form of art. It is usually created in _____ places, such as on buildings or fences. Graffiti artists paint, draw, or write in these areas to _____ their ideas. Some artists use their real names, but others use fake names to make their art more _____. People used to think graffiti was a social problem, but it's now seen as a form of modern art. The work of graffiti artists can even be seen in art _____.

Vocabulary

B Choose the correct word for each definition.

celebrate	museum	fake	neighborhood	entire	express	growth

1 an area in a city or town: _____

2 to do something special on an important day or for an event: _____

3 having nothing left out: _____

4 untrue or unreal: _____

5 a building where artistic, cultural, or scientific items are shown: _____

6 to show a feeling or idea through words or actions: _____

• Before Reading   What do you know about prairie dogs?

Reading 1

Have you ever seen a prairie dog? Actually, I am one. We are a type of squirrel. We live in underground tunnels. Fruit and vegetables are our favorite foods. You can find prairie dogs almost everywhere in North America. We are very social and live in large groups of a few families. ⁵

Aren't you curious about why we are called prairie dogs? First, a prairie is a large area of flat, grassy land. That's where we live. Second, we are called dogs because of the barking sound we make. So why do we bark? ⓐ Well, we have many *predators, such as eagles and coyotes. ¹⁰ ⓑ When we feel danger from them, we bark loudly to warn our family and friends. ⓒ We like to spend time with our family and friends. ⓓ You can imagine how important our barking sound is. You may not believe me, but we make different sounds for different levels of danger.

*predator: an animal that kills and eats other animals

1 **What is the best title for the passage?**

① Why Wild Animals Live in Groups

② Interesting Facts about Prairie Dogs

③ What Are the Favorite Foods of Prairie Dogs?

④ What Kinds of Animals Live in American Prairies

2 **Which sentence is NOT needed in the passage?**

① ⓐ   ② ⓑ   ③ ⓒ   ④ ⓓ

3 **What is the best pair for blanks (A) and (B)?**

| People named prairie dogs after _____ (A) _____ and _____ (B) _____ . |

　　　　(A)　　　　　　　　　　(B)

① their predators   —   the way they run

② the homes they build   —   the food they eat

③ the place they live   —   the sound they make

④ their social lifestyles   —   the way they look

4 **According to the passage, a prairie dog makes a barking sound when** _____ .

5 **What is NOT mentioned in the passage?**

① where prairie dogs live

② what prairie dogs eat

③ how fast prairie dogs are

④ what prairie dogs' predators are

6 **What is mentioned about the barking of prairie dogs?**

① Only the strongest prairie dog in the family barks.

② Baby prairie dogs learn how to bark from their parents.

③ Prairie dogs' predators don't like their loud barking sound.

④ Prairie dogs make different barking sounds for different situations.

Prairie dogs live underground. Their homes are made up of many tunnels and rooms. They spend a lot of time and work really hard to make their homes. Each room has a different purpose. There are rooms for baby prairie dogs, rooms for sleeping, and even bathrooms! There ⁵ is also a special room near the entrance. Prairie dogs go there to listen and find out if dangerous animals are nearby. Sometimes other animals, such as owls and snakes, move into these homes and share them with the prairie dogs.

To summarize the passage, what is the best pair for blanks (A) and (B)?

| Prairie dogs live in ____(A)____ rooms, and they all have their own ____(B)____ . |

	(A)		(B)
①	special	—	bathroom
②	dark	—	entrance
③	safe	—	purpose
④	underground	—	purpose
⑤	large	—	entrance

Summary / Graphic Organizer

A Choose the correct words to fill in the blanks.

underground	danger	eagles	groups	live	dogs

Reading 1

Prairie dogs are a kind of squirrel. They live in _____ homes across North America. They eat mostly fruit and vegetables, and live in large _____. They're called "prairie dogs" for two reasons. First, the flat, grassy areas where they _____ are called prairies. And second, they bark just like _____. Prairie dogs use their barking to warn each other of _____.

Vocabulary

B Choose the correct word for each definition.

grassy	social	share	area	flat	bark	curious

1 a part of a city, town, country, etc: _____

2 not having any hills or mountains: _____

3 to have or use something with others: _____

4 living together or enjoying life in groups: _____

5 interested to know about something: _____

6 to make a short, loud sound like a dog does: _____

• Before Reading   What is the most interesting musical you've seen?

Dear Diary,

Today I went to the Royal Theater with my parents to see the musical *The Lion King*. Its story comes from an animated movie: A young lion becomes the king after a long journey with his friends. I read that 75 million people around the world have seen the musical since it started on Broadway. <u>I'm so happy to be among them!</u>

The performance was simply amazing. It was full of beautiful costumes, wonderful acting, and great dancing. ⓐI counted 25 different kinds of animals, birds, fish, and insects. ⓑThe most surprising ones were the giraffes. ⓒGiraffes' long necks are useful when they eat leaves from trees. ⓓThey were over five meters tall! Of course, my favorite animal was Simba, the lion king.

The songs were fantastic too. Most of them were written by Elton John. My favorite song was "Hakuna Matata." It means "no worries" in Swahili. It's a great song, and it really makes me happy!

I thanked my parents for taking me to such a wonderful show. I want to see it again someday.
Good night!

1 **What is the diary mainly about?**

① a trip to see a musical

② a plan to visit Broadway

③ a day at the movie theater

④ an audition for a performance

2 **What is the meaning of the underlined sentence?**

① I want to see the musical on Broadway.

② I'm glad to have seen the popular musical.

③ I'd like to see a musical performed by many people.

④ I'm happy to have seen a musical with so many people.

3 **Which sentence is NOT needed in the passage?**

① ⓐ   ② ⓑ   ③ ⓒ   ④ ⓓ

4 **What does "Hakuna Matata" mean?**

_____

5 **What is NOT true about the musical _The Lion King_?**

① It will be made into an animated movie.

② It shows how a young lion becomes the king.

③ It includes many different kinds of animals.

④ Elton John wrote most of its songs.

6 **Which best describes the writer's feeling in the diary?**

① proud

② bored

③ afraid

④ excited

The person behind the amazing appearance of the musical *The Lion King* is the director and costume designer, Julie Taymor. While growing up, she studied acting. (ⓐ) Later she traveled around the world to learn about dolls and ⁵ costumes. (ⓑ) Using these experiences, she designed the costumes for *The Lion King*. (ⓒ) So, she designed beautiful African costumes and amazing animal masks for their heads. (ⓓ) Taymor's idea was very successful. ¹⁰ (ⓔ) And she later won many awards, such as the Tony Award for Original Costume Design.

Where would the following sentence best fit?

| But she didn't want the actors to hide inside big animal costumes. |

① ⓐ   ② ⓑ   ③ ⓒ   ④ ⓓ   ⑤ ⓔ

Summary / Graphic Organizer

A   Choose the correct words to fill in the blanks.

written	enjoyed	won	costumes	someday	animated

Reading 1

The writer of the diary went to see *The Lion King*. It's a musical based on a(n) _____ movie about a lion. Millions of people have already seen the musical. The writer _____ it and really loved the beautiful costumes. His favorite character was Simba, the lion. He also enjoyed the songs, many of which were _____ by Elton John. His favorite was "Hakuna Matata," which means "no worries" in Swahili. He hopes to see the musical again _____.

Reading 2

We can thank Julie Taymor for the amazing African _____ and animal masks in *The Lion King* musical.

Vocabulary

B   Choose the correct word for each definition.

director	insect	surprising	journey	useful	appearance	hide

1   the act of traveling from one place to another: _____

2   a small animal, such as a fly or an ant, which has six legs: _____

3   a person who controls a movie or play: _____

4   able to help you when you want to do or get something: _____

5   to be in a place so you can't be found or seen: _____

6   how someone or something looks: _____

UNIT 06 Psychology

• Before Reading Do you have any special tips for remembering things?

Do you have trouble remembering things? Then try using the Zeigarnik effect. Because of it, people remember unfinished tasks better than finished ones.

Bluma Zeigarnik discovered the effect when she was at a restaurant one day. She saw that waiters remembered long, unpaid orders, but forgot them after they were paid for. To find out the reason, Zeigarnik tried an experiment. People were asked to do a series of tasks. Before they were done with the tasks, she would suddenly force half of them to do something else. This experiment showed that people remembered the unfinished tasks around 90% better than the finished ones.

But why does this happen? Zeigarnik believes that an unfinished task stays in a person's mind. So the person has to finish the task to stop thinking about it. When the task is done, that person won't need to remember it anymore. So then, it becomes easier to forget.

You can use this effect when you study. Instead of _____(A)_____, schedule some breaks into your study time. This will help you improve your memory!

28

1   **What is the passage mainly about?**

① tips to finish work faster

② good manners at a restaurant

③ how to stop thinking too much

④ why unfinished work is easier to remember

2   **What is NOT true about Zeigarnik's experiment in the passage?**

① She wanted to find out the reason for the waiters' behavior.

② In the experiment, she asked people to do a series of tasks.

③ 90% of people in the experiment did something else before they finished the tasks.

④ Whether they finished the task or not affected their memory.

3   **To stop thinking about the task, the person** _____

_____.

4   **The 3rd paragraph suggests that when a task is done,**

_____.

① it is easily forgotten

② people try to remember it

③ it stays in a person's mind

④ people keep thinking about it

5   **What is the best choice for blank (A)?**

① finishing all at once

② learning something new

③ thinking about other work

④ remembering everything in the book

6   **Write T if the statement is true and F if it's false.**

(1) The Zeigarnik effect is named after the person who discovered it.

(2) Waiters remembered long, unpaid orders until they were paid for.

IT'S ALL ABOUT ME

It's easier to remember information related to us. Our brain thinks about and stores this information differently. So the more you can relate the information to yourself, the better ⁵ you can remember it. This was proved through research. One study had people look at a list of adjectives—smart, shy, etc. However, they had to think about the words in a different way. The first group decided whether each word described their personality. The second group decided whether each word was long. Later, everyone was asked to use ¹⁰ the words again in a surprise task. Though the first group remembered the words well, the second group didn't. So the next time you want to remember something, try _____ the information to yourself.

What is the best choice for the blank?

① asking

② proving

③ changing

④ describing

⑤ connecting

Unit Review

Summary / Graphic Organizer

A   Choose the correct words to fill in the blanks.

tasks   mind   themselves   experiments   forgotten   unpaid

Reading 1

People remember unfinished _____ better than finished ones. This is called the Zeigarnik effect. It was discovered by Bluma Zeigarnik. At a restaurant, she saw that waiters remembered _____ orders but forgot about paid orders. To learn more, she tried an experiment. She found that people remembered unfinished tasks about 90% better than finished tasks. This happens because unfinished tasks stay in your _____ until you finish them. But finished tasks are _____ because you don't need to remember them anymore.

Reading 2

People can easily remember information related to _____.

Vocabulary

B   Choose the correct word for each definition.

discover   describe   prove   adjective   behavior   connect   order

1   a word that gives information about someone or something: _____

2   to find or learn about something, especially for the first time: _____

3   to explain someone or something in words: _____

4   to show something is true by presenting facts: _____

5   to join something with something else: _____

6   how someone acts: _____

• Before Reading   Have you had problems with bad breath?

Reading 1

Dear Dr. Kay,

Whenever I talk to my roommate, she gives me chewing gum. At first I thought she was just being nice. But now I'm worried it is because of my bad breath. I'm so embarrassed! What can I do?   5

Sabrina

Bad breath is a pretty common problem. (ⓐ) Sometimes it is caused by smelly food like onions and garlic. (ⓑ) Bacteria love to eat food between the teeth. (ⓒ) After eating, their number increases. (ⓓ) In fact, most people have over 10 billion bacteria in their mouth.   10 That's a lot! When these bacteria die, they smell bad. This is the smell that causes bad breath. For better breath, you should clean your teeth regularly. This will clean away the food pieces between your teeth. Another way is to clean your tongue too. Many bacteria live at the   15 back of the tongue. _____(A)_____, you should drink a lot of water. Water washes away mouth bacteria. Sweet drinks, however, will make your breath worse.   20 Sugar is mouth bacteria's favorite food! I hope these tips help you.

Dr. Kay

1 **What does Sabrina think her roommate means when she gives her chewing gum?**

① "Please excuse my bad breath."

② "I like to share everything with you!"

③ "Please refresh your breath with this."

④ "Please do not fall asleep during class."

2 **What is Dr. Kay mainly talking about? (Choose two.)**

① the reasons for bad breath

② changing bad eating habits

③ ways to improve your breath

④ the right way of brushing your teeth

3 **Where would the following sentence best fit?**

But most often it is caused by bacteria in the mouth.

① ⓐ   ② ⓑ   ③ ⓒ   ④ ⓓ

4 **Who is most likely to have bad breath?**

① "I brush my teeth three times a day, every day!"

② "When I brush my teeth, I clean my tongue too."

③ "I like water more than juice. I drink water often."

④ "I love drinking soda. It makes my mouth feel fresh."

5 **What is the best choice for blank (A)?**

① Firstly   ② Finally

③ However   ④ Luckily

6 **According to the passage, what is NOT true?**

① Foods like onions and garlic make your breath smell bad.

② Bacteria eat the food between our teeth and then grow in number in our mouth.

③ We have bad breath because of dead bacteria in our mouth.

④ It's hard to find bacteria at the back of the tongue.

Do you often have bad breath in the morning? Many people wake up with a bad taste and smell in their mouth.

(A) This is good news for your mouth bacteria. When you go to bed each night, your mouth bacteria stay awake to eat! 5

(B) The reason has to do with *saliva. Saliva is very useful. It washes away mouth bacteria. It even kills many bacteria. But while you sleep, your mouth makes less saliva.

(C) Overnight, millions of them die and start to smell. The result is bad morning breath. Quick, find your 10 toothbrush!

*saliva: the liquid that is made in your mouth

Choose the best order of (A), (B), and (C) after the given text.

① (A) – (C) – (B)
② (B) – (A) – (C)
③ (B) – (C) – (A)
④ (C) – (A) – (B)
⑤ (C) – (B) – (A)

Summary / Graphic Organizer

A Choose the correct words to fill in the blanks.

water	smelly	common	regularly	sweet	dead	bacteria

Reading 1

Question: I have bad breath. What causes it? And what can I do about it?

▼

Answer:

1. Reasons for bad breath
   - _____ food
   - bacteria in the mouth - over 10 billion in most people's mouth
     - smell bad when _____
2. Tips for good breath
   - Clean your teeth _____.   • Clean your tongue.
   - Drink a lot of _____.   • Avoid _____ drinks.

Reading 2

Saliva usually washes away smelly mouth _____, but overnight they die and make your mouth smell bad.

Vocabulary

B Choose the correct word for each definition.

breath	awake	tongue	roommate	cause	common	result

1 someone who you share a room or house with: _____

2 the air you take in and let out of your nose or mouth: _____

3 not sleeping: _____

4 to make something happen: _____

5 something that happens because of another thing: _____

6 often happening to many things or people: _____

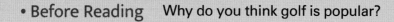

Reading 1

Golf has been played for hundreds of years. But no one is sure who invented it. Most people believe it was started in Scotland in the 12th century. Back then, shepherds often became bored while watching their sheep. So they invented a game: They pushed stones into rabbit holes with sticks. ⁵ This game soon became popular throughout the country. Even <u>the king of Scotland</u> started playing it! In the 17th century, golf was introduced to other countries such as France, Germany, and England.

Nowadays, there are golf ¹⁰ courses all around the world. (ⓐ) And more than 60 million people enjoy playing it. (ⓑ) Firstly, golfers can enjoy natural beauty and fresh air. (ⓒ) This is very relaxing for people who live in crowded cities. (ⓓ) Secondly, it ¹⁵ is _____(A)_____. Generally, golf courses are pretty long, so golfers need to walk a lot. Swinging a club also makes a golfer's upper body strong.

1 **What is the best title for the passage?**

① A Shepherd Who Enjoyed Golf

② Scotland: The Land of Modern Golf

③ How Was Golf Introduced to the World?

④ Golf: A Sport That's Been Loved for Centuries

2 **Why does the writer mention the king of Scotland?**

① to show how popular golf was

② to explain how golf came to Scotland

③ to give an example of a famous golfer

④ to suggest that golf was a game for the rich

3 **What is NOT true about golf?**

① It is not clear who invented it.

② Stones and sticks were used to play it at first.

③ It started as a way of hunting rabbits.

④ It was played in European countries in the 17th century.

4 **Where would the following sentence best fit?**

But why is it so popular?

① ⓐ   ② ⓑ   ③ ⓒ   ④ ⓓ

5 **What is the best choice for blank (A)?**

① a slow game

② tiring exercise

③ great exercise

④ a natural game

6 **Write T if the statement is true and F if it's false.**

(1) Playing golf is refreshing for people who live in the city.

(2) People like golf because golf courses are usually short.

What do you think golf balls are made of? The earliest golf balls were made out of wood. They could only travel about 100 meters. Later, golfers made balls out of chicken feathers covered in leather. These could travel a little farther. In the 19th century, factories began to make golf balls out of rubber and plastic. ⓐInterestingly, golfers found that scratched up balls traveled farther. ⓑIt took them up to 30 days to make a golf ball, though. ⓒSo they started making little holes in them. ⓓToday, hundreds of dimples are put in each golf ball at the factory. ⓔMost golf balls have around 250 to 450 dimples, and they can travel about 270 meters!

Which sentence is NOT needed in the passage?

① ⓐ   ② ⓑ   ③ ⓒ   ④ ⓓ   ⑤ ⓔ

Summary / Graphic Organizer

A Choose the correct words to fill in the blanks.

| dimples   exercise   spread   shepherds   crowded   enjoyed |

Reading 1

Golf

In Early Days
- possibly invented by bored Scottish _____
- became more popular and _____ to other countries

In Modern Days
- _____ by more than 60 million people around the world
- gives city people a chance to get fresh air and _____

Reading 2

Many different golf balls have been made in the past, but balls with _____ in them travel farthest.

Vocabulary

B Choose the correct word for each definition.

| shepherd   relaxing   crowded   push   introduce   scratch   leather |

1 to make someone or something move forward: _____

2 too full of people or things: _____

3 someone whose job is taking care of sheep: _____

4 to damage the surface of something: _____

5 making you feel less stressed and more rested: _____

6 to bring something new into use: _____

• Before Reading   Have you ever done any volunteer work?

Reading 1

We all know that there's no place like home. But sadly, there are many people without homes. Habitat for Humanity builds houses for these poor people. It is a charity which started in 1976. Using volunteer workers, it builds new houses all around the world. 5

There are two important rules at Habitat. First, the homes are not free. The homeowners have to pay for them. The money is then used when Habitat builds other homes. Of course, the price is very cheap. Second, the owners have to help the volunteers build their new homes. There is 10 _____(A)_____ for these rules. Habitat knows that homeowners feel pleased and proud when they pay for and build their own homes.

Homeowners are not the only ones who feel good about the new homes. The volunteers who work at Habitat also feel proud. This is because they know their work can change other people's lives. In the end, everyone's life is better thanks to Habitat 15 for Humanity.

1 What is the best title for the passage?

① New Homes for Volunteers

② Habitat: A Lesson for the Poor

③ What Makes Volunteers Proud?

④ Habitat: Building Homes and Hope

2 What does Habitat make new homeowners do? (Choose two.)

① help build their houses

② pay for their new houses

③ work as volunteers for other homes

④ move to another house after some time

3 What is NOT mentioned about Habitat for Humanity?

① who it works for

② when it started

③ how many houses it built

④ how it uses homeowners' money

4 What is the best choice for blank (A)?

① a right way   ② a big change

③ a good reason   ④ an old example

5 Volunteers feel happy about their work because they know that

_____.

6 Write T if the statement is true and F if it's false.

(1) The houses Habitat builds are not expensive.

(2) Habitat hopes that homeowners sell their houses to poor people.

Volunteer vacations are not like usual vacations. Instead of just spending time at the beach, you do some volunteer work. This means you can enjoy helping others while you travel. There are many kinds of volunteer vacations. So you can easily find one to match your personality. If you have a lot of energy, you might like to help build houses for poor people. If you love kids, you 5 could teach poor children at a school or help sick children in a hospital. Volunteer vacations can be hard work, but the feeling of helping others is a wonderful gift.

To summarize the passage, what is the best choice for blanks (A) and (B)?

Volunteer vacations let you enjoy ___(A)___ others in a way that ___(B)___ your personality.

	(A)		(B)
①	helping	—	matches
②	helping	—	builds
③	finding	—	shows
④	teaching	—	matches
⑤	teaching	—	builds

Summary / Graphic Organizer

A   Choose the correct words to fill in the blanks.

proud	volunteers	cheap	poor	free

Reading 1

Habitat for Humanity is a charity. Since 1976, it has built houses for _____ people. The homes aren't _____, but they are not expensive. Habitat asks the owners to pay for their new houses. They also have to help Habitat build the house. There is a reason for this. When the house is finished, the homeowners feel _____. The _____ who help build it also feel happy. Habitat makes everyone feel good!

Vocabulary

B   Choose the correct word for each definition.

charity	rule	proud	usual	habitat	humanity	volunteer

1   where a wild animal or plant lives: _____

2   all the people living in the world: _____

3   someone who does a job without being paid: _____

4   a group of people that gives money or help to poor or sick people: _____

5   feeling pleased about something that you own or have done: _____

6   a clear guide on what someone can or cannot do in situation: _____

• **Before Reading**   Have you ever read *Anne of Green Gables*?

Reading 1

At school one day, Diana pointed to a new boy. "That's Gilbert Blythe. He just returned from visiting his cousins. He's handsome! But be careful because he's a big brat."

Soon, Anne saw Gilbert tie another girl's hair to her chair. "That's mean!" thought Anne. 5

Then Gilbert tried to make Anne look at him. But Anne was looking out the window. She pictured herself taking a walk by the beautiful lake. At that moment, Gilbert pulled her hair from behind.

"Your hair is the same color as carrots," he laughed. 10 "Carrots! Carrots!"

Anne jumped from her chair. "You are a mean, hateful boy," she shouted. Then—smack!—she broke her *slate over Gilbert's head. All the students in the room were surprised. Their teacher was very mad. For punishment, Anne had to stand in the corner. Gilbert tried to explain that it was all his _____(A)_____. But that didn't matter to the 15 teacher.

After class, Gilbert told Anne he was sorry. Anne didn't look at Gilbert. She acted like she didn't hear him.

*slate: a small blackboard used in place of a notebook in the past

1 **What is the best title for the story?**

① Boring Days at School

② Anne Gets into Trouble

③ One Fine Day with Gilbert

④ Gilbert Becomes Anne's Friend

2 **Based on the story, what is most likely the meaning of the phrase "a big brat"?**

① someone who often misses classes

② someone who is very popular in school

③ someone who enjoys looking out the window

④ someone who likes to play tricks on other people

3 **What was Anne's punishment for fighting in class?**

_____

4 **What is the best choice for blank (A)?**

① joy   ② plan   ③ fault   ④ lesson

5 **Which best describes Anne's feelings in the underlined sentence?**

① shy   ② sorry

③ angry   ④ excited

6 **Write T if the statement is true and F if it's false.**

(1) Gilbert bothered Anne while she was daydreaming.

(2) Anne thought "carrots" was an interesting nickname.

Lucy Maud Montgomery, the writer of *Anne of Green Gables*, was born in 1874 in Canada. After her mom's death, Montgomery was sent to her grandparents' home while she was still a baby. Her childhood there gave her many ideas for *Anne of Green Gables*.

Her imagination grew as she played outdoors and listened to her grandfather's stories. Later, she worked as a teacher but dreamed of becoming a writer. When she created the character of Anne in 1905, however, publishers weren't interested. This disappointed Montgomery, so she put the story away in an old hat box. But a few years later, she tried again. And in 1908, *Anne of Green Gables* was finally published. After that, Montgomery wrote many more popular stories about Anne. Over a century later, her books still touch the hearts of people worldwide.

What is NOT true about Lucy Maud Montgomery?

① She grew up with her grandparents.

② Spending time outdoors and listening to stories made her imaginative.

③ Before being a writer, she used to be a teacher.

④ It took her 10 years to publish her first story about Anne.

⑤ She made up several stories using the character Anne.

Summary / Graphic Organizer

A Choose the correct words to fill in the blanks.

mean   angry   writer   handsome   fault   moment

Reading 1

Diana warns Anne about Gilbert Blythe, the new boy in class. He is _____ but bratty. Anne can tell he is a(n) _____ boy when she sees him play a trick on another student. When Anne is not looking, Gilbert pulls her hair and teases her about her red hair. Anne is so _____ that she hits his head with her slate. The teacher tells Anne to stand in the corner even though Gilbert says it is his _____. Gilbert tries to say sorry, but Anne pretends not to hear him.

Reading 2

Lucy Maud Montgomery's dream of becoming a successful _____ came true through her character Anne.

Vocabulary

B Choose the correct word for each definition.

tie   childhood   mean   character   cousin   publisher   explain

1 a person or a company that makes books or magazines: _____

2 a child of your uncle or aunt: _____

3 unkind and rude to others: _____

4 to give a reason for something that happens: _____

5 someone who appears in a book, play, film, etc.: _____

6 to attach two ends of a long material by making a knot: _____

Reading 1

New Zealand is famous for kiwis. But what exactly are kiwis?

The original kiwi is a small brown bird. This bird is native to New Zealand. It has a round body, small wings, and short feathers. It can't fly. There used to be a lot of kiwis in 5 New Zealand. But now there are only a few thousand left.

Kiwi is also the word for a person from New Zealand. The reason is that the kiwi bird is New Zealand's national animal. So, when New Zealanders go overseas, they are often called "Kiwis." 10

You probably already know the last kind of kiwi — the fruit. But can you guess why it's called a kiwi? It's because the fruit is grown in New Zealand and looks like a kiwi bird. Like the bird, it's small, round, and covered in short brown hair. But in New 15 Zealand, it's called a "kiwifruit," not a "kiwi." That way, people don't get _____(A)_____ between the bird, the people, and the fruit!

1 **What is the best title for the passage?**

① It's Time to Have Fun with Kiwis

② New Zealand: The Country of Kiwis

③ The Natural Beauty of New Zealand

④ Kiwis: The New Hope for New Zealand

2 **What is NOT true about kiwi birds?**

① They live in New Zealand.

② They are round with small wings.

③ They fly higher than other birds.

④ Their numbers have become smaller.

3 **Why are people from New Zealand called "Kiwis"?**

It's because _____ .

4 **What is the best choice for blanks (B) and (C)?**

| The kiwifruit got its name from _____(B)_____ and _____(C)_____ . |

	(B)		(C)
①	where it grows	—	how it looks
②	who grows it	—	what it helps
③	when it grows	—	who sells it
④	how it grows	—	when it is eaten

5 **What is the best choice for blank (A)?**

① bored   ② curious   ③ confused   ④ interested

6 **According to the passage, the three types of kiwis are**

_____ .

① old and natural

② famous but weird

③ small but important

④ different but related

We cannot think of New Zealand without thinking of the Maori, the native people of New Zealand. They sailed there from Polynesia 1,000 years ago and started living in small groups all over the country.

5

(A) But the Maori survived. Today there are more than 875,000 Maori people in New Zealand, and their culture and language are still important.

(B) Each group developed its own history and culture. In the nineteenth century, the British arrived in New Zealand. They wanted to control New Zealand, so they made an agreement with the Maori leaders.

10

(C) They promised to protect the Maori way of life. For many years, though, the Maori had a hard time. They died from diseases and in wars with the British. They lost most of their land in the wars as well.

Choose the best order of (A), (B), and (C) after the given text.

① (A) – (C) – (B)

② (B) – (A) – (C)

③ (B) – (C) – (A)

④ (C) – (A) – (B)

⑤ (C) – (B) – (A)

Summary / Graphic Organizer

A Choose the correct words to fill in the blanks.

kiwifruit	flightless	feather	survive	brown	person

Reading 1

Kiwis in New Zealand

The Bird	- small, brown, _____ bird found in New Zealand - not very many left
The People	- meaning a _____ from New Zealand - nickname that comes from the kiwi bird
The Fruit	- small and _____ like the kiwi bird - grown in New Zealand - called a _____ by New Zealanders

Reading 2

Though the British fought to control New Zealand, the native Maori and their culture and language still _____ today.

Vocabulary

B Choose the correct word for each definition.

sail	cover	agreement	national	overseas	protect	native

1 to put one thing over another: _____

2 to travel across water in a boat or ship: _____

3 related to a country across the sea: _____

4 a promise or decision made by two or more people: _____

5 living or growing naturally in a place: _____

6 to keep from getting hurt, injured, or lost: _____

• Before Reading   Are you interested in a vegan diet?

Reading 1

Vegan diets have become popular recently for improving one's health. But you should think about the benefits and problems with a vegan diet before you try one yourself.

Luca

There are many health benefits to a vegan diet. Plant-based foods decrease the risk of many ⁵ serious diseases. Researchers even found that vegans have a lower risk of weight and heart problems.

Maeve

Vegans often have a hard time getting vitamins D and B12. Plant-based foods also don't offer enough calcium or iron. They are mostly found in ¹⁰ meat.

Nova

Cow farms harm the environment by producing a large amount of greenhouse gases. _____(A)_____, plants do not produce a lot of greenhouse gases. So a vegan diet can help fight against global warming.

Finn

You have to be very diligent to be a vegan. ⓐThis is because you must read ¹⁵ the labels on food all the time. ⓑThese labels should tell us information about food. ⓒIf you don't, you won't get the necessary vitamins and minerals. ⓓYou also might need to take pills with vitamins and minerals in them.

1   **What is the best title for the passage?**

    ① What Should You Do to Become a Vegan?

    ② What Is Good and Bad about a Vegan Diet?

    ③ Is a Vegan Diet the Answer to Global Warming?

    ④ Do Vegans Really Have a Lower Risk of Gaining Weight?

2   **Why does Luca think vegan diets are good?**

    ① They cut calories for weight loss.

    ② They have foods full of calcium and iron.

    ③ They lower the risk of many health problems.

    ④ They provide necessary vitamins and minerals.

3   **Because calcium, iron and some vitamins are mostly found in meat, vegans _____.**

4   **What is the best choice for blank (A)?**

    ① However

    ② Therefore

    ③ In addition

    ④ For example

5   **Which sentence is NOT needed in the passage?**

    ① ⓐ   ② ⓑ   ③ ⓒ   ④ ⓓ

6   **Who has the same opinion as the following statement?**

A vegan diet can have a good impact on the earth.

    ① Luca   ② Maeve   ③ Nova   ④ Finn

Do you want to start a vegan diet but you're worried about giving up some of your favorite foods? Well, don't worry! There are non-meat foods that often taste and even look like real meat! Tofu, a soft food made from soy milk, is one such type of non-meat food. (ⓐ) It contains many basic proteins. (ⓑ) So, instead of eggs, you can eat tofu. (ⓒ) Certain vegetables, such as ⁵ mushrooms, lentils, and chickpeas, can also replace the meat you eat. (ⓓ) You can enjoy your favorite foods by eating vegetables instead! (ⓔ) So, why don't you give it a try?

Where would the following sentence best fit?

> When these vegetables are mixed with plant oil or wheat gluten, they can be turned into meat-like foods.

① ⓐ　　　　② ⓑ　　　　③ ⓒ　　　　④ ⓓ　　　　⑤ ⓔ

Summary / Graphic Organizer

A Choose the correct words to fill in the blanks.

difficult	risk	greenhouse	replace	harm	labels

Reading 1   Opinions on the Vegan Diet

Agree

Luca: It lowers the _____ of serious diseases and health problems.

Nova: It slows down global warming by reducing _____ gases from cow farms.

Disagree

Maeve: It's _____ to get enough vitamin D, vitamin B12, calcium, and iron.

Finn: It makes us always check _____ on food and take pills for vitamins and minerals.

Reading 2

Foods such as tofu and certain vegetables can be used to _____ meat.

Vocabulary

B Choose the correct word for each definition.

diet	replace	weight	taste	popular	benefit	diligent

1 liked by many people: _____

2 the food and drink someone usually eats and drinks: _____

3 to use one thing instead of another: _____

4 how heavy a person or thing is: _____

5 something that has a good or helpful effect: _____

6 showing care and a lot of effort in doing something: _____

• Before Reading   What do you know about Abraham Lincoln?

Reading 1

Abraham Lincoln was a famous US president. _____(A)_____ Some say it was because he was such a good politician. Others say it was because he was very intelligent. But maybe there's another reason. It could be the advice he got from an eleven-year-old girl!   5

In 1860, Lincoln was running for president. A girl named Grace Bedell liked Lincoln's ideas. She wanted him to win. One day, she was looking at a picture of Lincoln. The shadows in her room covered part of his skinny face, and it looked good. So she decided to write Lincoln a letter of   10
advice. She said his skinny face looked funny, but it would look better with a beard. Then people would like him more.

What happened next? Lincoln grew a beard, and later that year he was elected president! ⓐBefore long, he visited Grace's town. ⓑHe liked to travel by train. ⓒHe wanted to meet the girl who had given him such special advice.   15
ⓓEveryone in the town was surprised by the president's visit. They had no idea a little girl could _____(B)_____!

1 **What is the passage mainly about?**

① a letter sent by mistake

② a gift from the president

③ advice for Abraham Lincoln

④ Lincoln's relationship with others

2 **What is the best choice for blank (A)?**

① Then how did he look?

② But why was he elected?

③ So how did he become so rich?

④ And who was his favorite president?

3 **What was Grace's advice for Lincoln?**

① You should run for president next time.

② Growing a beard will make you more popular.

③ If you change your style, you will look slimmer.

④ Always smile if you want to look nice and kind.

4 **Which sentence is NOT needed in the passage?**

① ⓐ   ② ⓑ   ③ ⓒ   ④ ⓓ

5 **What is the best choice for blank (B)?**

① change history

② fight for freedom

③ upset the president

④ become a politician

6 **Write T if the statement is true and F if it's false.**

(1) Grace didn't like Lincoln, because he was too skinny.

(2) Lincoln did not follow Grace's advice in the end.

When Abraham Lincoln was a young man, he got his nickname "Honest Abe." He became well-known for his personality while working in a store. One evening, while counting the
5 store's money, Lincoln found that he had a few cents too many. He found out that he had given a customer too little change. That night, he walked a few miles to return the money to the customer. Another time, Lincoln thought
10 that he had given a woman too little tea for her money. So he carried some more tea to her house. Later, Lincoln became president of the US, and it is said that he never told a lie in his life.

What is the best title for the passage?

① The Great Fortune Earned from Honesty

② Unknown Stories about Past US Presidents

③ How Young Lincoln Overcame His Hard Times

④ A Young Man's Dream That Changed the Nation

⑤ How Being Truthful Brought about Lincoln's Nickname

Summary / Graphic Organizer

A Choose the correct words to fill in the blanks.

shadow	beard	helped	skinny	advice	personality

Reading 1

In 1860, Abraham Lincoln was trying to become the president of the United States. An eleven-year-old girl saw his picture and thought his _____ face looked funny. She thought he would look a lot better with a(n) _____. So she sent him a letter and suggested that he grow one. He took her _____ and was soon elected president! Later, he visited her town to meet the little girl who had _____ him so much.

Reading 2

Abraham Lincoln is known as "Honest Abe" due to famous stories of his _____ while working as a store worker and the president.

Vocabulary

B Choose the correct word for each definition.

return	politician	skinny	carry	change	lie	elect

1 to give or send something back: _____

2 someone who works as a member of the government: _____

3 something that you say or write when you know it is not true: _____

4 the money you receive when you pay too much for something: _____

5 very thin or narrow, sometimes in a bad way: _____

6 to choose someone for a position by voting: _____

The Economy

• **Before Reading**   What do coins in your country look like?

Do you have any coins in your pocket? Take one out and look at it closely. It's round, right? Do you know why most coins are round? Here's why.

First of all, they're easy to use in daily life. You can pick up and hold round coins without worrying about sharp ⁵ corners. Because there aren't any corners, the coins are safe and can't hurt people. ⓐ In addition, they work well with machines. ⓑ Machines should be replaced regularly. ⓒ Round coins can roll, so they can be easily moved in vending machines and coin-sorting machines. ⓓ This ¹⁰ means that they won't get stuck in a machine. Furthermore, they are less likely to wear down. Coins are made to last for a long time. Corners often rub against things, so they wear down quicker. However, a round coin doesn't have <u>this problem</u>. Finally, round shapes are _____(A)_____ produced in factories. Circles are simpler than other shapes, so they're faster to make. Therefore factories can make many round ¹⁵ coins at the same time.

1 What is the best title for the passage?

① Let's Roll the Coins!

② Who Invented the First Coin?

③ Why People Use Round Coins

④ How We Can Use Coins Longer

2 Which sentence is NOT needed in the passage?

① ⓐ   ② ⓑ   ③ ⓒ   ④ ⓓ

3 Round coins are easy to use in daily life because you can

_____ .

4 What does this problem refer to?

① Coins easily roll in machines.

② Coins take a long time to make.

③ Corners are expensive to make.

④ Corners rub and wear down faster.

5 What is the best choice for blank (A)?

① hardly

② mostly

③ easily

④ slowly

6 What is NOT suggested in the passage?

① Round coins are safer to pick up.

② Round coins function well with machines.

③ Coins without corners don't last as long as other shapes.

④ Round shapes are better for making coins in large amounts.

These days, people often use their credit or debit card to buy things. But there are some great reasons to use cash too. First of all, cash is accepted by all sellers. Businesses need a special device for payments by credit or debit card. So, some smaller shops and restaurants only take cash. In addition, using cash can _____. When paying with a card, it's common to spend ⁵ more money. But with cash, you can see how much money you have. So it is harder to spend lots of money. Paying with money is great for both sellers and buyers!

What is the best choice for the blank?

① help you spend less

② make you save change

③ help you buy better things

④ give you a discount at shops

⑤ stop you from losing your card

Summary / Graphic Organizer

A Choose the correct words to fill in the blanks.

wear down	machines	spending	make	round	corners

Reading 1

Question	Why are coins _____?
▼	
Answer	1. They're easy and safe to use in daily life.
	2. They work well with _____.
	3. They're less likely to _____.
	4. They're easy and fast to _____ in factories.

Reading 2

It can be good to shop with cash because all sellers accept it, and using it can stop you from _____ too much money.

Vocabulary

B Choose the correct word for each definition.

function	discount	sort	roll	invent	sharp	reason

1 an amount taken off the usual price of something: _____

2 to create or produce something new: _____

3 having a fine edge or point: _____

4 a cause or an explanation for something: _____

5 to put things in order or into groups based on their features: _____

6 to move by turning over and over again: _____

• **Before Reading**   Have you ever visited a special festival?

Reading 1

The song words "Up, up, and away, my beautiful, my beautiful balloon!" describe how the people at the Albuquerque International Balloon Fiesta feel about their floating wonders. Held in New Mexico, USA, it's the world's largest hot air balloon festival. For nine days in early ⁵ October, the fiesta offers an unforgettable experience to visitors from all over the world.

The most popular event is watching all the balloons lift off. Imagine 700 baskets with big, colorful balloons. Then, all together like an orchestra, their burners roar and they ¹⁰ all rise. <u>Not enough to take your breath away?</u> Then give the Evening Balloon Glow a try. The glowing balloons look like fireflies flying in the evening sky. What else can <u>these beauties</u> do? They can race to see which can travel the farthest.

ⓐIn addition to the balloon shows, there are many other events to enjoy. ⓑYou can listen to live music and visit the Balloon Discovery Center. ⓒThe history ¹⁵ of balloons isn't very long. ⓓAnd if you really do want to go up, up and away, take a balloon ride!

1 **What is the passage mainly about?**

① balloon races at big festivals

② the popularity of balloon rides

③ the world's largest balloon festival

④ popular tourist sites in Albuquerque

2 **When and for how long is the Albuquerque International Balloon Fiesta held?**

It is held in _____.

3 **Why does the writer use the underlined sentence?**

① to say that 700 balloons are not enough to fill the sky

② to introduce other interesting events that you can enjoy

③ to show that watching the balloons rise is not so interesting

④ to advise you to take a deep breath before you watch the balloons

4 **What do these beauties refer to?**

① baskets   ② fireflies

③ balloons   ④ burners

5 **Which sentence is NOT needed in the passage?**

① ⓐ   ② ⓑ   ③ ⓒ   ④ ⓓ

6 **Who is NOT talking about his or her experience at the fiesta?**

① Charlie: Hundreds of colorful balloons filled the sky.

② Laura: I took pictures of glowing balloons in the evening sky.

③ Paul: It was exciting to see balloons racing each other.

④ Jennifer: The contest for the most beautiful balloon was very popular.

Would you like to fly through the air in a balloon? Then visit Cappadocia in Turkey! It's an amazing place for hot air balloon rides.

(A) But the best reason to ride a balloon in Cappadocia is the landscape. It's full of beautiful valleys, dark caves, and hidden cities. No wonder thousands of tourists go to Cappadocia every year! 5

(B) Besides the great weather, Cappadocia also has a lot of open space for balloons. There are many places to explore, and there isn't any wildlife. Therefore, the balloons can fly high in the sky or close to the ground.

(C) One reason is because it has excellent weather. Balloons need calm weather to fly, and Cappadocia is nice almost all year round. In fact, balloons can fly on about 250 days each year there! 10

Choose the best order of (A), (B), and (C) after the given text.

① (A) – (C) – (B)

② (B) – (A) – (C)

③ (B) – (C) – (A)

④ (C) – (A) – (B)

⑤ (C) – (B) – (A)

Summary / Graphic Organizer

A Choose the correct words to fill in the blanks.

| glowing | describe | rise up | held | largest | landscape |

Reading 1

The Albuquerque International Balloon Fiesta is the _____ balloon festival in the world. It is _____ in New Mexico, USA, for nine days every October. Hundreds of balloons all _____ together, filling the sky with their beautiful colors. There is also an evening balloon event, with _____ balloons floating through the night sky. And there are balloon races too. Besides the balloon shows, there are many fun activities for people to enjoy at this wonderful festival.

Reading 2

Cappadocia in Turkey is a great place to ride hot air balloons because it has calm weather, lots of space, and an amazing _____.

Vocabulary

B Choose the correct word for each definition.

| wonder | landscape | tourist | weather | wildlife | glow | discovery |

1 the area of land you can see from one place: _____

2 animals and plants that live in nature: _____

3 to produce a soft, continuous light: _____

4 the act or process of finding or being found: _____

5 a person who visits a place for fun: _____

6 what the sky and air outside are like at a time and place: _____

The Environment

Reading 1

On the last Saturday of March, something strange happens. The lights go out for one hour in cities all over the world! But it isn't an accident. It is an event called Earth Hour.

Earth Hour started in 2007. It was planned by the World ⁵ Wide Fund for Nature (WWF). The WWF is a group that tries to protect the environment. ⓐThey asked people to turn off their lights for one hour. ⓑSpending a day without lights is not as easy as we think. ⓒFewer lights mean less energy is used. ⓓAnd using less energy means ¹⁰ less pollution is created. The first Earth Hour was a big success, and now there's one every year.

Some people think Earth Hour is silly. They say one hour isn't long enough to make a difference. Of course, they're right. But Earth Hour is _____(A)_____ . It shows people that saving energy is important. It also shows that they can make a ¹⁵ difference by working together. One person's small choices can have a big effect throughout the world.

1 **What is the best title for the passage?**

① One Special Hour for the Earth

② Experience a Day in the Wild

③ A New Holiday around the World

④ An Accident That Became a Holiday

2 **Which sentence is NOT needed in the passage?**

① ⓐ   ② ⓑ   ③ ⓒ   ④ ⓓ

3 **What is the best choice for blank (A)?**

① a rule   ② a promise

③ a behavior   ④ a symbol

4 **Why don't some people like Earth Hour?**

① because most pollution comes from driving cars

② because saving energy for one hour is not helpful

③ because lots of accidents can happen in dark cities

④ because it's too uncomfortable to live without lights

5 **What is NOT true about the passage?**

① The WWF got the idea for Earth Hour by accident.

② People turn off their lights for an hour during Earth Hour.

③ The first Earth Hour in 2007 was very successful.

④ Earth Hour happens once a year.

6 **Which of the following best shows the idea behind Earth Hour?**

① The walls have ears.

② Bad news travels fast.

③ No news is good news.

④ Many drops make an ocean.

The World Wide Fund for Nature (WWF) is a group that works for the environment. It started in Switzerland in 1961 and now has more than 5 million members in more than 100 countries. The WWF's goal is to stop damage to the environment and protect all plants and animals. To do so, it protects natural places so that animals can continue to live there. It also encourages ⁵ governments to protect animals from hunters and other dangers. Most importantly, the WWF teaches people around the world to keep the earth clean and beautiful for the future.

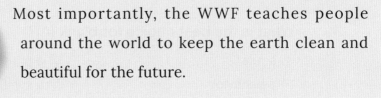

To summarize the passage, what is the best choice for blanks (A) and (B)?

The WWF works with people around the world to ___(A)___ environmental damage and ___(B)___ plants and animals against danger.

	(A)		(B)
①	save	—	put
②	stop	—	protect
③	help	—	find
④	build	—	guard
⑤	protect	—	destroy

Summary / Graphic Organizer

A Choose the correct words to fill in the blanks.

turn off	together	protect	held	symbol

Reading 1

Earth Hour

- started by the World Wide Fund for Nature (WWF) in 2007
- now _____ every year

- asks people to _____ their lights for one hour

- a _____ of saving energy and working _____

Vocabulary

B Choose the correct word for each definition.

goal	choice	throughout	save	fund	encourage	pollution

1 in every part of something: _____

2 something that you hope to do in the future: _____

3 to make someone do something by giving good reasons to do it: _____

4 to use less of something so you can use some of it later: _____

5 an option that you pick: _____

6 the act of damaging the earth's air, water, and land, etc.: _____

Reading 1

Smoke detectors, MRI, and running shoes — what do all these inventions have in common? It may sound strange, but they were all made possible by space research.

(ⓐ) NASA does research to create new technologies and products for their space program. (ⓑ) One example ⁵ is smoke detectors. (ⓒ) They were first used in the space station in 1973 to detect any dangerous gases. (ⓓ) Now smoke detectors are used in most homes and buildings to warn people of fire. NASA also developed ways to make the signals sent from spacecraft clearer. Thanks to this ¹⁰ technology, doctors now have MRI. Also, the material for running shoes came from the special boots for astronauts. It lessens the shock from running.

Some people say NASA spends too much money on its space research. And it's true that its research costs billions of dollars every year. But NASA's work doesn't just stay in space. People on Earth get to use it too, sometimes every day. ¹⁵

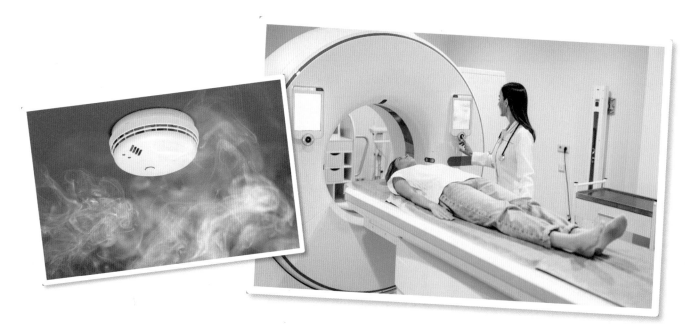

1 What is the best title for the passage?

① Building a Better Spacecraft

② Daily Life inside a Spaceship

③ The History of Space Research

④ Space Research: Used on Earth

2 How does the writer introduce the topic?

① by asking how to use some products

② by talking about common products in our life

③ by explaining how much money NASA spends

④ by showing which products are useful in space

3 Where would the following sentence best fit?

> But this research also creates products we can use on Earth.

① ⓐ ② ⓑ ③ ⓒ ④ ⓓ

4 Smoke detectors were first created to detect _____

_____ .

5 The 3rd paragraph suggests that space research _____ .

① is expensive but useful

② should cost less money

③ will increase competition among countries

④ shows how much money was used by NASA

6 Write T if the statement is true and F if it's false.

(1) NASA invented MRI to help cure serious illnesses.

(2) The running shoes we wear today come from space research.

(3) NASA spends billions of dollars every year on its research.

Here are two students' opinions on space research.

Sabrina

There are many serious problems here on Earth. So it doesn't make sense to spend billions of dollars on space research. Thousands of people die of hunger every day. Some people say we can get useful resources from space. But there are resources here on Earth that aren't ⁵ used enough yet. Why don't we spend money on solar energy and wind energy instead?

José

Most importantly, _____. After many years, Earth may become too hot and too crowded to live on. So we should keep using space research to look for other places to live in ¹⁰ space. Also, curiosity is the start of all science. Without it, we might still be living in caves! Our curiosity helps us do amazing things.

What is the best choice for the blank?

① humans must plan for the future

② space research costs less than before

③ we need to learn more about energy sources

④ scientists should test the safety of spaceships

⑤ humans caused environmental problems on Earth

Summary / Graphic Organizer

A Choose the correct words to fill in the blanks.

device	clearer	shock	astronauts	dangerous

Reading 1

How We Benefit from NASA's Space Research

Example 1: smoke detectors warning people of fire

• used to detect _____ gases in the space station

Example 2: MRIs for doctors

• make signals from spaceships _____

Example 3: the material for running shoes

• originally made for the special boots of _____

• lessens the _____ from running

Vocabulary

B Choose the correct word for each definition.

serious	daily	astronaut	lessen	solar	signal	warn

1 to tell someone about a possible problem or danger: _____

2 happening every day: _____

3 someone who travels to and works in space: _____

4 to make something become smaller, weaker, or less important: _____

5 extremely bad or dangerous: _____

6 an action or sound used to give information: _____

Technology

Reading 1

We need energy to live. Luckily, we can find it everywhere! It's in sunlight, water, and wind. It's even found under our feet!

The earth is filled with energy—or, heat. But its surface often moves. So the heat often escapes through its surface. ⓐ<u>It</u> heats up water near the surface of the earth. Some of this heated water is brought to a power plant and made into steam. The steam turns a fan with a generator on ⓑ<u>it</u>. Now, we have electricity!

There are many good reasons to use geothermal energy. First, the weather doesn't affect ⓒ<u>it</u> because the earth is always releasing heat. But windmills need wind and solar panels need _____(A)_____ to work effectively. Secondly, geothermal plants are small. They require less land than other plants. So they can be easily moved to ideal locations.

Geothermal energy isn't used much yet. However, ⓓ<u>it</u>'s good for us and the earth. Remember, <u>we can find treasure beneath our feet!</u>

5

10

15

1 **What is the best title for the passage?**

① The Energy Hidden Beneath Our Feet

② Sunlight: The Next Energy Source for All

③ The Dangers of Using Geothermal Energy

④ How Geothermal Energy Harmed the Earth

2 **Which is NOT referring to the same thing?**

① ⓐ 　　　② ⓑ 　　　③ ⓒ 　　　④ ⓓ

3 **Put the following in the correct order.**

The earth's surface moves and allows heat to escape.
→ ____(A)____ → ____(B)____ → ____(C)____

(1) (A) • 　　　• ⓐ The heat warms up water near the earth's surface.

(2) (B) • 　　　• ⓑ A fan powered by steam creates electricity.

(3) (C) • 　　　• ⓒ The heated water is made into steam.

4 **What is NOT mentioned as a benefit of geothermal energy?**

① It can be generated in any weather.

② It doesn't release bad materials.

③ Plants don't take up a lot of space.

④ Plants are easy to move to other areas.

5 **What is the best choice for blank (A)?**

① thick fog 　　　② heavy rain

③ clear skies 　　　④ a flash of lightning

6 **What can be inferred from the underlined sentence?**

① Geothermal energy is very hard to see.

② Geothermal energy is a precious resource.

③ We cannot use geothermal energy anymore.

④ We can use geothermal energy in the underground.

Since 2011, around 6.8 million people have left their homes because of the Syrian civil war. These people have difficulty finding electricity. However, a company called WakaWaka is helping by giving them small solar-powered devices.

WakaWaka's "Power" device runs on solar energy. With one full day of charging, it can provide 150 hours of bright light. It can also power cell phones and other electronic devices. ⓐ Thanks to this, people can contact their friends and family. ⓑ Then they can tell more people about the greatness of the device. ⓒ WakaWaka has already given 25,000 Power devices to Syrians in need. ⓓ The company has also started a "buy one, give one" campaign. ⓔ Every time a Power device is bought, WakaWaka will donate another one.

Which sentence is NOT needed in the passage?

① ⓐ   ② ⓑ   ③ ⓒ   ④ ⓓ   ⑤ ⓔ

Summary / Graphic Organizer

A Choose the correct words to fill in the blanks.

| electricity | heat | weather | device | windmills | escape |

Reading 1

People need energy to live. And we can find it in the earth. The earth is filled with
_____. The earth's surface moves and lets it _____. We
call it geothermal energy. It heats water near the surface of the earth. We take some
of this water and turn it into steam at power plants. The steam turns a fan with a
generator. This makes _____. Geothermal energy isn't affected by
_____. Also, geothermal plants are small. So they can be moved easily.
Geothermal energy is good for the earth and us.

Reading 2

Because of WakaWaka's solar-powered _____, thousands of Syrian
families now have light and electricity.

Vocabulary

B Choose the correct word for each definition.

| contact | device | steam | release | location | danger | treasure |

1 the chance of getting hurt or killed: _____

2 to make a call or write to another person: _____

3 a thing that is made for a certain purpose: _____

4 to let something go so it can move or act freely: _____

5 the hot air from boiling water: _____

6 a place, area, or position: _____

The Arts

Reading 1

Famous artwork is very expensive. But it also has an important cultural value. So when it's moved from museum to museum for international shows, people have to be very, very careful. Usually it takes more than three months to plan the move. 5

_____(A)_____ First, the box is usually left at the museum for 24 hours before being packed. This ensures that the air inside the box is the same as the air in the museum. Also, the boxes, trucks, and planes are all designed not to shake the art. They even have special 10 climate controllers inside. This way, the works experience _____(B)_____ from being moved. Lastly, there are security guards. They keep the priceless art from being stolen. ⓐOf course, important artwork must still be insured. ⓑIf it is very valuable, the insurance can be very high. ⓒIt's not easy to decide who pays for the insurance. ⓓA great work such as the *Mona Lisa* might be insured for 15 millions of dollars!

All of this sounds very difficult. But it lets us see great artwork at museums near our homes.

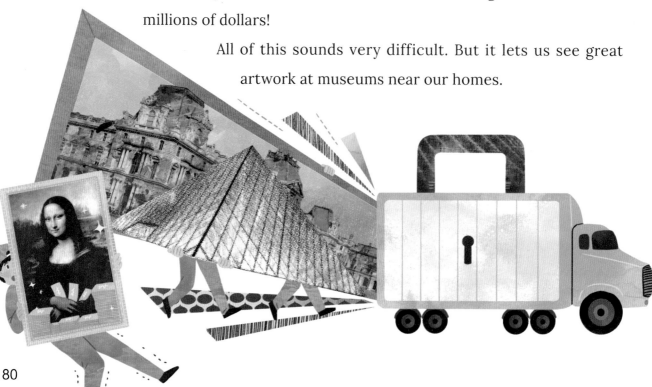

1   **What is the passage mainly about?**

① moving valuable artwork

② what makes art so valuable

③ interesting jobs at museums

④ protecting artwork from thieves

2   Famous artwork should be moved with care because it's not only

expensive but also _____ .

3   **What is the best choice for blank (A)?**

① Why is some artwork so expensive?

② Then what makes moving artwork so difficult?

③ What is the most important thing at art shows?

④ So what should be done to send artwork overseas?

4   **What is the best choice for blank (B)?**

① special shows

② terrible shaking

③ the least change

④ different seasons

5   **Which sentence is NOT needed in the passage?**

① ⓐ   ② ⓑ   ③ ⓒ   ④ ⓓ

6   **What is NOT true about the passage?**

① Planning the movement of artwork can take three months or more.

② Boxes for famous artwork are specially made right before packing.

③ Security guards make sure the artwork is safe during the move.

④ Artwork with a high value needs very expensive insurance.

"No Flash Photography Allowed!" Most art museums don't want visitors to use the camera flash when they take pictures. But why? Camera flashes can hurt paintings! It sounds strange, but it's true. A camera flash creates heat and light. Heat and light can damage the canvas that the painting is on. They can even damage the paint itself. Of course, one camera flash cannot hurt a ⁵ painting. But museums are worried about the effect of many flashes over many years. If everyone uses flash photography, the effect will be great. After a long time, <u>it'll be like leaving the painting out in the sun!</u>

What is the meaning of the underlined sentence?

① the painting can be displayed outdoors

② sunlight helps visitors enjoy the painting

③ drying the painting regularly is necessary

④ the weather affects how much the painting is damaged

⑤ camera flashes can be as bad as sunlight for the painting

Summary / Graphic Organizer

A Choose the correct words to fill in the blanks.

plan	controllers	shake	flash	careful	thieves

Reading 1

Famous artwork is very valuable. So people must be _____ when it is moved from museum to museum. It takes months to _____ each move. The air inside the box must be the same as the air in the museum. Also, it is important to make sure the artwork doesn't _____ too much during the move. Finally, security guards are needed to protect the artwork from _____. The artwork must also be insured. A painting like the *Mona Lisa* could be insured for millions of dollars.

Reading 2

Museums do not allow _____ photography because it can damage the painting over time.

Vocabulary

B Choose the correct word for each definition.

value	experience	allow	pack	hurt	climate	shake

1 to let someone do or have something: _____

2 the type of weather in a place: _____

3 the importance or usefulness of something: _____

4 to make something move from side to side or up and down: _____

5 to cause pain or harm to someone: _____

6 to have something happen to you or affect you: _____

• **Before Reading** Can you imagine what the lives of slaves were like in the past?

Reading 1

Harriet Tubman was born a slave in the American state of Maryland in 1820. (ⓐ) In 1849, she successfully ran away. (ⓑ) She returned many times and helped hundreds of slaves escape to the north. (ⓒ) Because of her actions, she became known as the "Moses" of her people. (ⓓ)　5

When Tubman was a young child, she was beaten and whipped by her masters. One time, her owner threw a heavy object at another slave, but it hit her instead. It nearly crushed her head and left a deep scar. The injury caused Tubman health problems for the rest of her life.　10

Slave owners offered money to anyone who could catch Tubman. _____(A)_____, she bravely continued to help slaves become free. Neither she nor any of the slaves she helped were ever caught.

1 **What is the best title for the passage?**

① The History of American Slaves

② A Slave Who Escaped to Maryland

③ People Who Fought against Slavery

④ A Brave American Woman Who Saved Slaves

2 **Where would the following sentence best fit?**

Soon after, she went back to Maryland and saved her family.

① ⓐ   ② ⓑ   ③ ⓒ   ④ ⓓ

3 **Harriet Tubman was called "Moses" because she helped**

_____.

4 **What is the 2nd paragraph mainly about?**

① how brave Tubman was

② people who helped Tubman

③ Tubman's friendship with other slaves

④ the pain Tubman went through as a slave

5 **What is the best choice for blank (A)?**

① Sadly   ② Moreover

③ However   ④ In fact

6 **What is NOT true about Harriet Tubman? (Choose two.)**

① She was a slave in the state of Maryland in the US.

② She saved not only her family but also other slaves.

③ When escaping, she was injured by a heavy object.

④ In the end, she was caught and put in jail.

Harriet Tubman will be the new face of the American $20 bill. Tubman will be the first woman on the front of a US bill in over 100 years. She will replace Andrew Jackson, the seventh president of the United States. Jackson, who was a slave owner, will be moved to the back of the bill. ⓐPeople respect him because he allowed common men to vote. ⓑThe new bill will not appear right away. 5 ⓒIn fact, it may not appear until around the year 2030. ⓓStill, people are very excited about the change. ⓔThey admire the courage she had and her belief in equality.

Which sentence is NOT needed in the passage?

① ⓐ　　② ⓑ　　③ ⓒ　　④ ⓓ　　⑤ ⓔ

Summary / Graphic Organizer

A Choose the correct words to fill in the blanks.

| beat | replace | heavy | slave | left | save |

Reading 1

Harriet Tubman was a _____ in the American state of Maryland until she escaped in 1849. She returned to _____ her family and many other slaves and became known as the "Moses" of her people. When she was young, her masters whipped and _____ her. One day, she was hit in the head with a _____ object. This caused her to have health problems for the rest of her life. Although slave owners tried to catch Tubman, they never caught her or the slaves she helped.

Reading 2

Harriet Tubman will _____ Andrew Jackson on the new American $20 bill due to people's respect for her courage and beliefs.

Vocabulary

B Choose the correct word for each definition.

| scar | offer | nearly | continue | equality | beat | throw |

1 almost, but not completely: _____

2 a mark on the skin which is left after an injury: _____

3 to ask someone if they want to have or use something: _____

4 the same rights and responsibilities for every person: _____

5 to do something or to keep doing something without stopping: _____

6 to hit several times: _____

Photo credits

JUNIOR
READING EXPERT

A Theme-Based Reading Course for Young EFL Learners

Level 1

Answer Key

JUNIOR
READING EXPERT

A Theme-Based Reading Course for Young EFL Learners

Answer Key

Level **1**

UNIT *01* *Food*

pp.8-9

Reading 1

Before Reading Yes, I love sweets like chocolate and marshmallows!

1 ② **2** ② **3** ④ **4** ④ **5** ④ **6** put it on a cracker with chocolate

해석

마시멜로는 부드럽고 맛있는 간식이다. 그것들은 푸딩, 초콜릿 바, 그리고 다른 많은 후식에 사용된다. 그런데 '마시멜로'는 무엇을 의미할까? '마시멜로'라는 단어는 식물의 이름과 그것이 자라는 장소로부터 온다. 이 식물은 야생 아욱(mallow)이라고 불린다. 그것은 marsh라고 불리는 습지에서 자란다.

오래전, 그리스인들은 상처를 치료하기 위해 마시멜로를 사용했다. 그것들은 약과 같았다! 나중에 이집트인들은 그것들로 후식을 만들었다. 그들은 견과류와 꿀을 그것들에 섞었다. 그러나 현대의 마시멜로는 프랑스에서 왔다. 19세기에 프랑스의 사탕 가게 주인들은 아욱 식물의 뿌리를 설탕, 달걀 흰자, 그리고 물과 섞었다. 사람들은 그것들을 좋아했다! 그러나 그것들은 만드는 데 너무 오랜 시간이 걸렸고, 그래서 아욱 식물 대신에 젤라틴이 사용되었다. 이러한 이유로, 오늘날의 마시멜로에는 어떤 아욱 식물도 들어 있지 않다.

요즘, 사람들은 마시멜로로 스모어를 만드는 것을 아주 좋아한다. 이것을 만들기 위해서, 여러분은 마시멜로를 구워서 초콜릿과 함께 그것을 크래커 위에 올려놓는다. 그 이름은 "좀 더 주세요"를 의미한다. 그리고 하나 먹어보고 나면, 여러분도 더 많이 원할 것이다!

어휘

tasty ⑱맛있는 snack ⑲간식 dessert ⑲후식 wetland ⑲습지 marsh ⑲습지 heal ⑧치유하다, 낫게 하다 injury ⑲부상, 상처 medicine ⑲약 mix A with B A와 B를 섞다 nut ⑲견과류 owner ⑲주인 root ⑲(식물의) 뿌리 gelatin ⑲젤라틴 instead of ~ 대신에 nowadays ⑨오늘날 roast ⑧굽다 [문제] origin ⑲기원 spread ⑧퍼지다 season ⑲계절 get rid of ~을 제거하다 produce ⑧생산하다 by accident 우연히 past ⑲과거

구문 해설

6행 It grows in wetlands [**called** marshes].
- called marshes: wetlands를 수식하는 과거분사구

7행 Long ago, Greeks used marshmallows **to heal** injuries.
- to heal: '~하기 위하여'의 의미로 목적을 나타내는 부사적 용법의 to부정사

12행 But they took **too long to make**, so gelatin *was used* instead of the mallow plant.
- too + 형용사 + to-v: 너무 ~하여 …할 수 없다
- was used: '사용되다'라는 뜻으로 'be동사 + 과거분사' 형태의 수동태 (← candy store owners used gelatin ~.)

2

①

해석

우피 파이는 미국의 전통 후식이다. 그것은 두 개의 케이크 같은 쿠키 가운데 크림을 넣어 만들어진다. 이 크림은 보통 바닐라 맛이 나고, 초콜릿 쿠키가 일반적으로 사용된다. 하지만, 호박과 생강 쿠키도 사용될 수 있다. 우피 파이는 분명히 맛있는 간식이다. 그런데 그 특이한 이름은 어디에서 생겨났을까? 한 전설에 따르면, 아이들이 우피 파이 하나를 받았을 때 신이 난 아이들은 "우피(야호)!"라고 소리치곤 했다. 사람들은 오랫동안 우피 파이를 즐겨 오고 있고, 그것들은 오늘날 여전히 인기 있다. 실제로, 2011년에 우피 파이는 미국 메인 주의 공식적인 주 간식이 되기도 했다.

어휘

traditional ⑧전통적인   usually ⑨보통, 대개   flavored ⑧~의 맛[향기]이 나는   typically ⑨보통, 일반적으로   pumpkin ⑨호박   gingerbread ⑨생강 쿠키[케이크]   certainly ⑨틀림없이, 분명히   treat ⑨특별한 것[선물]; *간식   unusual ⑧특이한, 흔치 않은   legend ⑨전설   yell ⑧소리치다   whoopee ⑪야호, 우아   receive ⑧받다   official ⑧공식적인   [문제] beloved ⑧인기 많은   recipe ⑨조리법

구문 해설

7행   ..., excited children **would yell** "Whoopee!" when they received *one*.
- would + 동사원형: '~하곤 했다'의 의미로, 과거의 불규칙적인 습관을 나타냄
- one: a whoopie pie를 가리키는 대명사

Unit Review   p.11

A **Reading 1** wetlands, dessert, roots, modern   **Reading 2** delicious

B **1** tasty   **2** heal   **3** unusual   **4** legend   **5** spread   **6** medicine

Reading 2 해석

우피 파이는 미국 전역에서 수년간 맛있는 간식으로 즐겨져 왔다.

UNIT 02 Places

pp.12-13

Reading 1

Before Reading I love putting things together, and Legos are my favorite.

1 ② **2** ③ **3** ③ **4** ② **5** ④ **6** ②

해석

보고 싶은 욜란다에게

　나는 가족과 함께 덴마크에서 멋진 휴가를 보내고 있어. 오늘 우리는 레고랜드에 갔어. 그곳에 있는 모든 것은 레고 조각으로 만들어져 있었어, 5800만 개 이상의 레고 조각들로 말이야! 레고랜드 안에는 레고 블록들로 만들어진 몇 개의 작은 도시들이 있었어. 그것들은 귀엽고 완벽하게 만들어졌어. 그것들 옆에서 나는 거인같이 느껴졌지! 그다음에 우리는 레고랜드 사파리 공원을 방문했어. 잔디를 가로질러 햇빛 속을 걸으며 우리는 레고 블록들로 만들어진 야생 동물들을 보았어. 그것들은 진짜 같아 보였어. 엄마가 레고 사자 옆에서 내 사진을 찍어 주셨어. (내 사진기는 어디든지 들고 다닐 수 있을 만큼 작아.) 그 후에 우리는 놀이기구들을 탔어. 최고의 놀이기구는 Dragon Ride였어. 우리는 오랫동안 줄을 섰지. 우리가 마침내 줄 앞쪽에 이르렀을 때, 나는 정말 흥분되었어. 먼저 우리는 놀이기구를 타고 수천 개의 레고 조각으로 만들어진 성을 지나갔어. 성을 나오자 그 놀이기구는 롤러코스터가 되었어. 그것이 너무나 빨리 움직여서 엄마와 나는 비명을 질렀어! 나는 레고랜드로의 여행을 결코 잊지 못할 거야!

곧 보자.

켈리가

어휘

vacation 圏휴가　be made out of ~으로 만들어지다　piece 圏조각　million 圏백만의　inside 囡~ 안에　tiny 圏아주 작은　brick 圏벽돌; *(장난감용) 벽돌　perfectly 囝완벽하게　giant 圏거인　grass 圏풀, 잔디　sunshine 圏햇빛　wild 圏야생의　take one's picture ~의 사진을 찍다　enough 囝충분히　carry 图운반하다, 들고 다니다　go on a ride 놀이기구를 타다 (ride 圏놀이기구)　stand in line 줄을 서다　finally 囝마침내　reach 图~에 이르다　front 圏앞　excited 圏흥분한　through 囡~을 통과하여　castle 圏성　thousands of 수천의　travel 图여행하다; *움직이다　scream 图비명을 지르다　forget 图잊다　trip 圏여행　[문제] theme park 테마파크[유원지]　tour 圏관광　popular 圏인기가 많은　joyful 圏즐거운　bored 圏지루한　scared 圏무서운　interested 圏흥미를 가진

구문 해설

5행　Inside Legoland were some tiny cities [**made** out of Lego bricks].
　　　　부사구　　　　동사　　주어

- 장소의 부사구가 문장의 앞에 오면서 주어와 동사가 도치됨
- made ... bricks: some tiny cities를 수식하는 과거분사구

4

It traveled **so** fast **that** my mom and I screamed!

· so ~ that ...: 너무 ~하여 …하다

Reading 2 p.14

③

해석

레고 블록은 역사상 가장 성공한 장난감들 중 하나이다. 2000년에 그것은 '세기의 장난감'으로 뽑혔다. 그렇다면 왜 아이들은 레고를 그렇게 많이 좋아할까? 아마 그것은 레고가 그들로 하여금 상상력을 사용하게 하기 때문일 것이다. 아이들은 자신만의 창작물을 만들기 위해 레고 조각들을 조립할 수 있다. 레고라는 이름은 덴마크 단어인 'leg godt'에서 유래한다. 그것은 '잘 놀다'를 의미한다. 그리고 라틴어로 레고는 '내가 조립을 하다'라는 의미이다. 그것들이 만들어진 이후로 4,000억 개 이상의 레고 조각이 판매되었다. 그것은 전 세계 각 사람에게 62개 이상씩이라는 뜻이다!

어휘

successful 형 성공적인   history 명 역사   choose 동 선택하다   century 명 세기   perhaps 부 아마   put together 조립하다   own 형 자기 자신의, 고유한   creation 명 창작물   Danish 형 덴마크 (사람·말)의   since 접 ~한 이후로   more than ~ 이상의   billion 형 10억의   [문제] let 동 ~하게 하다   imagination 명 상상력

구문 해설

1행   The Lego brick is **one of the most successful toys** in history.

· one of + 최상급 + 복수명사: 가장 ~한 … 중 하나

5행   ... Lego **lets them use** their imagination.

· 사역동사(let) + 목적어 + 동사원형: ~가 …하게 하다

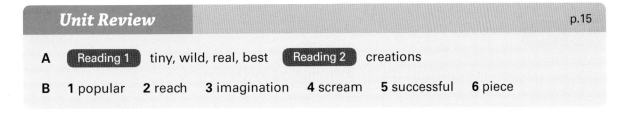

Unit Review p.15

A Reading 1 tiny, wild, real, best   Reading 2 creations

B **1** popular **2** reach **3** imagination **4** scream **5** successful **6** piece

Reading 2 해석

레고는 아이들이 블록을 조립함으로써 자신만의 창작물을 만들 수 있기 때문에 인기가 있다.

pp.16-17

Before Reading I have seen graffiti in my neighborhood before.

1 ② **2** ④ **3** ② **4** ③ **5** (1) F (2) T **6** express their thoughts to the world

해석

당신은 예술을 사랑하나요? 저는 그렇습니다. 저는 뉴욕의 그라피티 예술가입니다. 그라피티가 무엇일까요? 그것은 벽에 있는 색칠, 그림, 글쓰기와 같은 예술입니다. 보통, 그것은 건물이나 울타리 밖에서 행해집니다.

저는 그라피티를 그리기 위해 스프레이식 페인트, 마커, 스텐실을 사용합니다. 처음에, 저는 근처의 거리에 제 작품을 표현했습니다. 하지만 지금 저는 제 작업실에서 작업해요! 저는 작품을 완성한 후에 그것에 제 이름을 씁니다. 몇몇 그라피티 예술가들은 그들의 진짜 이름을 사용하지만, 저는 가짜 이름을 사용합니다. 저는 그것이 예술을 더 흥미롭게 만든다고 생각합니다. 저와 같은 그라피티 예술가들은 종종 그림 그리는 법을 독학합니다. 하지만 어떤 사람들은 예술 학교에 갑니다. 그라피티는 공공장소에서 행해지기 때문에, 사람들은 그것이 사회적인 문제라고 생각하곤 했습니다. 그러나 요즘, 그것은 현대 예술의 한 형태로 여겨집니다. 여러분은 심지어 그것을 미술관에서도 볼 수 있습니다!

다른 예술가들처럼, 그라피티 예술가들은 자신의 생각을 세상에 표현하기 위해 예술을 이용합니다. 그래서 저는 항상 제 작품을 뽐내는 것이 자랑스럽습니다.

어휘

graffiti 阌 (공공장소에 하는) 낙서, 그라피티   artist 阌 예술가   fence 阌 울타리   spray paint 스프레이식 페인트   stencil 阌 스텐실   neighborhood 阌 근처, 이웃   studio 阌 (방송국) 스튜디오; *작업실   artwork 阌 작품   fake 阌 가짜의   like 阠 ~와 같이, ~처럼   social 阌 사회의   form 阌 형태   modern art 현대 예술   gallery 阌 미술관   express 阍 표현하다   thought 阌 생각   show off 자랑하다   [문제] public 阌 공공의   private 阌 사적인   fabric 阌 직물, 천

구문 해설

9행   Graffiti artists, like me, often teach themselves **how to draw**.
　　　　　　주어　　　　　　　　　　　　동사　　간접목적어　　직접목적어

· how to-v: ~하는 방법

10행   Because graffiti is done in public spaces, people **used to think** it was a social problem.

· used to-v: ~하곤 했다 (과거의 습관이나 상태를 표현)

13행   Like other artists, graffiti artists use art **to express** their thoughts to the world.

· to express: '~하기 위하여'의 의미로 목적을 나타내는 부사적 용법의 to부정사

③

해석

그라피티의 중심에서

우리의 새로운 미술 전시회인 '그라피티의 중심에서'를 보러 오세요! 우리는 미술품을 거리에서 미술관 벽으로 가져올 것입니다. 여러분은 벽 전체에서 판화, 사진, 조각, 그리고 대형 작품들과 같은 100점 이상의 예술 작품들을 볼 수 있습니다. 그라피티가 인기 있는 현대 예술 형태로 성장한 것을 기념하기 위해 우리와 함께하세요!

일반 정보
· 언제: 2024년 5월 ~ 9월
· 어디에서: 브루클린 박물관 (뉴욕 브루클린 센트럴 스트리트 100)

티켓 가격

성인	$22
고령자 (65세 이상)	$16
학생	$14
어린이 (4세 – 12세)	$10

관람 시간

요일	시작	종료	마지막 입장
월요일 – 수요일	12:00 a.m.	7:00 p.m.	6:00 p.m.
목요일 – 금요일	11:00 a.m.	8:00 p.m.	7:00 p.m.
주말	10:30 a.m.	8:30 p.m.	7:30 p.m.

이 경험에 대한 더 많은 정보는 www.atthecenterofgraffiti.com을 참조하십시오.

어휘

bring 图 가져오다   piece 圆 조각; *(작품의) 한 점   print 圆 판화   sculpture 圆 조각   entire 圆 전체의   celebrate 图 기념하다   growth 圆 성장   museum 圆 박물관   entry 圆 입장   information 圆 정보   experience 圆 경험   [문제] hold 图 잡다; *(회의·시합 등을) 열다

구문 해설

2행   We're bringing art **from** the streets **to** our gallery walls.
       · from A to B: A에서 B로

Unit Review   p.19

A   Reading 1   public, express, interesting, galleries

B   **1** neighborhood   **2** celebrate   **3** entire   **4** fake   **5** museum   **6** express

그라피티는 예술의 한 형태이다. 그것은 보통 건물이나 울타리와 같은 공공장소에서 만들어진다. 그라피티 예술가들은 그들의 생각을 표현하기 위해 이 영역에 칠하거나, 그리거나, 글을 쓴다. 어떤 예술가들은 그들의 진짜 이름을 사용하지만, 다른 예술가들은 그들의 예술을 더 흥미롭게 만들기 위해 가짜 이름을 사용한다. 사람들은 그라피티가 사회적인 문제라고 생각하곤 했지만, 지금은 그라피티가 현대 예술의 한 형태로 여겨진다. 그라피티 예술가들의 작품은 미술관들에서도 볼 수 있다.

UNIT 04 Animals

Reading 1   pp.20-21

Before Reading I've seen them in the zoo before. They looked like squirrels.

1 ②　**2** ③　**3** ③　**4** it feels danger from predators　**5** ③　**6** ④

해석

여러분은 프레리도그를 본 적이 있나요? 사실 내가 프레리도그에요. 우리는 일종의 다람쥐에요. 우리는 땅속 굴에 살아요. 과일과 채소는 우리가 가장 좋아하는 음식이죠. 여러분은 북미의 거의 어디서나 프레리도그를 발견할 수 있어요. 우리는 사회성이 매우 좋으며 몇몇의 가족으로 이루어진 큰 무리를 지어 살아요.

왜 우리가 프레리도그라고 불리는지 궁금하지 않나요? 첫째, 프레리(prairie)는 평평하고 풀이 많은 땅을 가진 넓은 지역이에요. 바로 우리가 사는 곳이죠. 둘째, 우리는 우리가 내는 짖는 소리 때문에 도그(dog)라고 불려요. 그러면 우리가 왜 짖냐고요? 음, 우리에게는 독수리와 코요테 같은 많은 포식 동물들이 있어요. 우리가 그들로부터 위험을 느끼면 우리는 우리 가족과 친구들에게 경고하기 위해 큰 소리로 짖어요. (우리는 가족 및 친구들과 함께 시간을 보내는 것을 좋아해요.) 여러분은 우리의 짖는 소리가 얼마나 중요한지 상상할 수 있을 거예요. 여러분은 제 말을 믿지 않을 수도 있겠지만, 우리는 서로 다른 위험의 정도에 따라 다른 소리를 낸답니다.

어휘

prairie 몡초원　squirrel 몡다람쥐　underground 휑지하의 튀지하에(서)　tunnel 몡굴, 터널　social 휑사교적인 curious 휑궁금한　area 몡지역　flat 휑평평한　grassy 휑풀이 많은　bark 통짖다　eagle 몡독수리　coyote 몡코요테　danger 몡위험　loudly 튀큰 소리로　warn 통경고하다　[문제] name A after B B의 이름을 따서 A의 이름을 짓다　lifestyle 몡생활방식

구문 해설

6행　Aren't you curious about **why we *are called* prairie dogs**?
- why 이하는 전치사 about의 목적어 역할을 하는 간접의문문으로 '왜 ~인지'의 의미임
- are called: '(~라고) 불리다'라는 의미의 수동태 (← people(they) call us prairie dogs)

Second, we are called dogs because of <u>the barking sound</u> [(that) we make].

• we make 앞에 목적격 관계대명사 which 또는 that이 생략되어 있음

..., we bark loudly **to warn** our family and friends.

• to warn: '~하기 위하여'의 의미로 목적을 나타내는 부사적 용법의 to부정사

Reading 2   p.22

④

해석

프레리도그는 땅속에서 산다. 그들의 집은 많은 굴과 방으로 이루어져 있다. 그들은 집을 짓기 위해 많은 시간을 보내고 정말 열심히 일한다. 각 방은 서로 다른 목적을 가진다. 새끼 프레리도그를 위한 방과 잠을 자기 위한 방, 그리고 심지어 욕실도 있다! 입구 가까이에는 또한 특별한 방이 있다. 프레리도그는 위험한 동물들이 근처에 있는지 듣고 알아내기 위해 그곳으로 간다. 때때로 올빼미와 뱀 같은 다른 동물들이 이들 집으로 들어와 프레리도그와 집을 같이 쓰기도 한다.

어휘

be made up of ~으로 이루어져 있다   purpose ⑲목적   entrance ⑲입구   nearby ⑭근처에   owl ⑲올빼미
share ⑧공유하다

구문 해설

6행   Prairie dogs go there **to listen and find out** *if dangerous animals are nearby.*

• to listen and find out: '~하기 위하여'의 의미로 목적을 나타내는 부사적 용법의 to부정사

• if 이하는 listen and find out의 목적어로 사용된 명사절이며, 이때의 if는 접속사로 '~인지'의 의미임

Unit Review   p.23

A **Reading 1** underground, groups, live, dogs, danger

B **1** area **2** flat **3** share **4** social **5** curious **6** bark

Reading 1 해석

프레리도그는 일종의 다람쥐이다. 그들은 북미 전역의 땅속 집에 산다. 그들은 주로 과일과 채소를 먹고, 큰 무리를 지어 산다. 그들은 두 가지 이유로 '프레리도그'라고 불린다. 첫째, 그들이 사는 평평하고, 풀로 덮인 지역이 프레리(초원)라고 불린다. 그리고 둘째, 그들은 마치 개처럼 짖는다. 프레리도그는 서로에게 위험을 경고하기 위해 짖는 소리를 이용한다.

Before Reading I went to see *Beauty and the Beast* with my parents. I really loved the music.

1 ①   **2** ②   **3** ③   **4** It means "no worries."   **5** ①   **6** ④

해석

일기장에게

　　오늘 나는 부모님과 함께 뮤지컬 '라이언 킹'을 보기 위해 로열극장에 갔어. 그것의 줄거리는 애니메이션 영화로부터 왔어. 어린 사자가 친구들과의 오랜 여정 후 왕이 된다는 내용이지. 나는 그 뮤지컬이 브로드웨이에서 시작된 이후 전 세계 7,500만 명의 사람들이 그것을 관람했다고 읽었어. 내가 그들 중 한 명이라 아주 기분이 좋아!

　　공연은 아주 놀라웠어. 그것은 아름다운 의상과 훌륭한 연기 그리고 멋진 춤으로 가득 차 있었어. 나는 25가지 종의 다양한 동물들과 새, 물고기, 곤충의 수를 셌어. 가장 놀라운 것은 기린들이었어. (기린들의 긴 목은 나무의 나뭇잎을 먹을 때 유용해.) 그것들은 5미터가 넘었지! 물론 내가 가장 좋아하는 동물은 라이언 킹인 심바였어.

　　노래들도 환상적이었어. 곡의 대부분은 엘튼 존에 의해 쓰였어. 내가 가장 좋아하는 노래는 '하쿠나 마타타'였지. 그것은 스와힐리어로 '걱정하지 마'란 뜻이야. 그것은 멋진 노래이고 나를 정말 행복하게 만들어 줘!

　　나는 부모님께 그렇게 멋진 뮤지컬에 데리고 가 주셔서 감사하다고 했어. 나는 언젠가 그것을 다시 보고 싶어. 잘 자!

어휘

diary 몡일기   animated 휑애니메이션으로 된   journey 몡여행, 여정   million 휑백만의   among 쩐~ 중의 하나인 performance 몡공연 (perform 통공연하다)   simply 뷔단순히; *아주   amazing 휑놀라운, 굉장한   be full of ~으로 가득 차다   costume 몡의상   acting 몡연기   count 통(수를) 세다   insect 몡곤충   surprising 휑놀라운   useful 휑유용한   fantastic 휑환상적인, 멋진   worry 몡걱정   someday 뷔언젠가   [문제] audition 몡오디션   include 통포함하다

구문 해설

3행   Its story comes from an animated movie: A young lion becomes the king after a long journey with his friends.
　　• 콜론(:) 이하의 내용은 Its story에 대한 구체적인 내용임

5행   I read that 75 million people around the world **have seen** the musical since it started on Broadway.
　　• have seen: '경험'을 나타내는 현재완료

7행   I'm so happy **to be** among them!
　　• to be: '~해서, ~하니'의 의미로 감정의 원인을 나타내는 부사적 용법의 to부정사

③

해석

뮤지컬 '라이언 킹'의 놀라운 모습 뒤에 있는 사람은 감독이자 의상 디자이너인 줄리 테이머이다. 성장하면서 그녀는 연기를 공부했다. 이후 그녀는 인형과 의상에 대해 배우기 위해 전 세계를 여행했다. 이런 경험들을 이용하여, 그녀는 '라이언 킹'의 의상들을 디자인했다. 그러나 그녀는 배우들이 큰 동물 의상들 속으로 숨는 것을 원치 않았다. 그래서 그녀는 아름다운 아프리카 의상들과 배우들의 머리 위에 쓸 수 있는 놀라운 동물 가면들을 디자인했다. 테이머의 아이디어는 매우 성공적이었다. 그리고 그녀는 그 후 독창적인 의상 디자인 부문으로 토니상과 같은 많은 상들을 받았다.

어휘

appearance 몡 모습   director 몡 감독   designer 몡 디자이너 (design 몡 통 디자인(하다))   successful 휑 성공적인
win 통 (상 등을) 수상하다   award 몡 상   original 휑 독창적인   [문제] actor 몡 배우   hide 통 숨다

구문 해설

10행   And she later won many awards, **such as** the Tony Award for Original Costume Design.
　　　　• A such as B: B와 같은 A

Unit Review p.27

A Reading 1 animated, enjoyed, written, someday   Reading 2 costumes
B **1** journey **2** insect **3** director **4** useful **5** hide **6** appearance

Reading 1 해석

일기의 글쓴이는 '라이언 킹'을 보러 갔다. 그것은 사자 한 마리에 관한 애니메이션을 토대로 한 뮤지컬이다. 수백만 명의 사람들이 그 뮤지컬을 이미 관람했다. 글쓴이는 그 뮤지컬을 즐겁게 봤고 아름다운 의상이 정말 마음에 들었다. 그가 가장 좋아하는 캐릭터는 사자 심바였다. 그는 또한 노래들도 좋아했는데, 노래들 중 많은 곡을 엘튼 존이 작곡했다. 글쓴이가 가장 좋아하는 노래는 '하쿠나 마타타'였는데, 이것은 스와힐리어로 '걱정하지 마'라는 뜻이다. 그는 언젠가 그 뮤지컬을 다시 보길 희망한다.

Reading 2 해석

우리는 뮤지컬 '라이언 킹'에서의 놀라운 아프리카 의상들과 동물 가면에 대해 줄리 테이머에게 감사할 수 있다.

UNIT 06 Psychology

Before Reading   I write down things to remember in my planner.

1 ④   **2** ③   **3** has to finish it   **4** ①   **5** ①   **6** (1) T (2) T

해석

당신은 어떤 것을 기억하는 데 문제가 있는가? 그렇다면 자이가르닉 효과를 사용해 보라. 그것 때문에, 사람들은 끝낸 일보다 끝내지 않은 일을 더 잘 기억한다.

블루마 자이가르닉은 어느 날 식당에 있을 때 그 효과를 발견했다. 그녀는 웨이터들이 길고, 지불되지 않은 주문들은 기억하지만, 지불된 후에는 그것들을 잊어버리는 것을 보았다. 그 이유를 알아내기 위해, 자이가르닉은 실험을 시도했다. 사람들은 일련의 과제들을 하도록 요구받았다. 그들이 그 과제들을 끝마치기 전에, 그녀는 갑자기 그들 중 절반에게 다른 것을 하도록 했다. 이 실험은 사람들이 끝내지 않은 과제들을 끝낸 과제들보다 약 90% 더 잘 기억한다는 것을 보여주었다.

하지만 왜 이런 일이 일어날까? 자이가르닉은 끝내지 않은 과제가 사람의 마음속에 남아있다고 믿는다. 그래서 그 사람은 그것에 대해 생각하는 것을 멈추기 위해 그 과제를 끝내야 한다. 그 과제가 끝나면, 그 사람은 더 이상 그것을 기억할 필요가 없을 것이다. 그러고 나면, 그것은 잊어버리기 쉬워진다.

당신은 공부할 때 이 효과를 사용할 수 있다. <u>모든 것을 한꺼번에 끝내는 것</u> 대신에 당신의 공부 시간에 약간의 휴식 시간을 잡아라. 그것은 당신의 기억을 향상시키는 데 도움을 줄 것이다!

어휘

task ⑲일, 과제   discover ⑧발견하다   unpaid ⑲아직 돈을 내지 않은, 미납의   order ⑲주문   forget ⑧잊다   experiment ⑲실험   a series of 일련의   suddenly ⑭갑자기   force ⑧~하게 만들다   stay ⑧그대로 있다   instead of v-ing ~하는 대신에   schedule ⑧일정을 잡다   break ⑲휴식 (시간)   improve ⑧개선하다, 나아지다   [문제] tip ⑲끝; *조언   manner ⑲방식; *(~s) 예의   behavior ⑲행동   affect ⑧영향을 미치다   at once 한꺼번에

구문 해설

1행	Do you **have trouble remembering** things?
	• have trouble v-ing: ~하는 데 어려움을 겪다
8행	People **were asked to do** a series of tasks.
	• be asked to-v: 'ask + 목적어 + to-v' 구문이 수동태가 된 것으로 '~하도록 요구받다'라는 의미임
9행	..., she would suddenly **force half of them to do** something else.
	• force + 목적어 + to-v: ~가 …하도록 강요하다

⑤

해석

우리와 관련된 정보를 기억하는 것은 더 쉽다. 우리의 뇌는 이 정보에 대해 다르게 생각하고 저장한다. 그래서 여러분이 그 정보를 여러분 자신과 더 많이 연관시킬 수 있을수록, 여러분은 그것을 더 잘 기억할 수 있다. 이것은 연구를 통해 증명되었다. 한 연구는 사람들로 하여금 형용사 목록(똑똑한, 수줍은 등)을 보게 했다. 하지만, 그들은 그 단어들에 대해 서로 다른 방식으로 생각해야 했다. 첫 번째 그룹은 각각의 단어가 그들의 성격을 묘사하는지를 결정했다. 두 번째 그룹은 각각의 단어의 길이가 긴지를 결정했다. 나중에, 모두가 그 단어들을 깜짝 과제에서 다시 사용하라고 요청받았다. 첫 번째 그룹은 그 단어들을 잘 기억했지만, 두 번째 그룹은 잘 기억하지 못했다. 그러므로 다음에 여러분이 무언가를 기억하고 싶을 때, 그 정보를 여러분 자신에게 연결해 보라.

어휘

information 영 정보   relate 동 관련시키다   brain 영 뇌   store 동 저장하다   prove 동 입증[증명]하다   adjective 영 형용사   describe 동 묘사하다   personality 영 성격   [문제] connect 동 연결하다

구문 해설

1행   **It's** easier **to remember** information related to us.
· It은 가주어이고, to remember 이하는 진주어로 '~하는 것'의 의미

4행   So **the more** you can relate the information to yourself, **the better** you can remember it.
· the + 비교급 ~, the + 비교급 ...: ~하면 할수록 더 …하다

8행   The first group decided **whether** each word described their personality.
· whether 이하는 동사 decided의 목적어로 쓰인 명사절로, 이때 whether는 if와 바꾸어 쓸 수 있음

Unit Review p.31

A   Reading 1   tasks, unpaid, mind, forgotten   Reading 2   themselves

B   **1** adjective   **2** discover   **3** describe   **4** prove   **5** connect   **6** behavior

Reading 1 해석

사람들은 끝낸 과제들보다 끝내지 않은 과제들을 더 잘 기억한다. 이것은 자이가르닉 효과라고 불린다. 그것은 블루마 자이가르닉에 의해 발견되었다. 식당에서, 그녀는 웨이터들이 지불되지 않은 주문들을 기억하지만 지불된 주문들에 대해서는 잊어버리는 것을 보았다. 더 많은 것을 알기 위해, 그녀는 실험을 시도했다. 그녀는 사람들이 끝내지 않은 과제들을 끝낸 과제들보다 약 90% 더 잘 기억한다는 것을 발견했다. 이 일은 끝내지 않은 과제들이 여러분이 그것들을 끝낼 때까지 여러분의 마음속에 남아있기 때문에 일어난다. 하지만 끝낸 과제들은 여러분이 그것들을 더 이상 기억할 필요가 없기 때문에 잊혀진다.

사람들은 <u>자신들</u>과 관련된 정보를 쉽게 기억할 수 있다.

UNIT 07 Science

Reading 1   pp.32-33

Before Reading I think so. I love food with garlics, and it seems to cause bad breath.

1 ③ **2** ①, ③ **3** ② **4** ④ **5** ② **6** ④

해석

케이 박사님께

　제가 룸메이트에게 말을 할 때마다 그녀는 언제나 제게 껌을 줘요. 처음에 저는 그 애가 그저 친절하려는 마음에서 그런 줄 알았어요. 그런데 이제 그것이 제 입 냄새 때문인 것 같아 걱정돼요. 저는 매우 창피해요! 어떻게 해야 하죠?

사브리나

　입 냄새는 매우 흔한 문제입니다. 때때로 그것은 양파나 마늘처럼 냄새가 나는 음식에 의해 유발되지요. <u>그러나 그것은 입속에 있는 세균들에 의해 가장 자주 유발됩니다.</u> 세균들은 치아 사이에 있는 음식을 먹는 것을 좋아합니다. (음식을) 먹은 후에는 세균의 수가 증가하지요. 사실 대부분의 사람들은 그들의 입속에 100억 개 이상의 세균을 갖고 있습니다. 참 많죠! 이 세균들이 죽으면 나쁜 냄새가 납니다. 이것이 입 냄새를 유발하는 냄새입니다. 더 나은 입 냄새를 위해서는 이를 규칙적으로 닦아야 합니다. 이것은 치아 사이에 있는 음식 조각들을 청소해 줄 겁니다. 다른 방법으로는 혀도 닦아 주는 것입니다. 많은 세균들이 혀 뒤쪽에 살고 있습니다. <u>마지막으로,</u> 당신은 많은 물을 마셔야 합니다. 물은 입속의 세균을 씻겨 보냅니다. 그러나, 단 음료수는 입 냄새를 더 악화시킬 겁니다. 설탕은 입속의 세균이 가장 좋아하는 음식이거든요! 이 조언들이 당신에게 도움이 되길 바랍니다.

케이 박사

어휘

roommate 몡룸메이트 (방을 같이 쓰는 사람)　chewing gum 껌　breath 몡숨, 호흡　embarrassed 혱당황스러운
pretty 凰매우, 아주　common 혱흔한, 보통의　cause 통유발하다　smelly 혱(고약한) 냄새가 나는　onion 몡양파
garlic 몡마늘　bacteria 몡세균 (bacterium의 복수형)　increase 통증가하다　billion 혱10억의　regularly
凰규칙적으로　clean away ~을 청소해 없애다　tongue 몡혀　wash away ~을 씻어 없애다　[문제] excuse 통용서하다
share 통함께 나누다　refresh 통상쾌하게 하다　fall asleep 잠들다　brush one's teeth 이를 닦다　soda 몡탄산음료
luckily 凰다행히도

2행 **Whenever** I talk to my roommate, she *gives me chewing gum*.

· whenever: ～할 때마다 (= every time)

· give A B: A에게 B를 주다

14행 Another way is **to clean** your tongue too.

· to clean: '～하는 것'의 의미로 be동사 is의 보어로 사용된 명사적 용법의 to부정사

19행 Sweet drinks, however, will **make your breath worse**.

· make + 목적어 + 형용사: ～을 …하게 만들다

Reading 2   p.34

②

해석

당신은 종종 아침에 입 냄새가 나는가? 많은 사람들은 불쾌한 맛과 냄새를 입에 지닌 채로 잠에서 깬다. **(B)** 그 이유는 침과 관련이 있다. 침은 매우 유용하다. 그것은 입속의 세균을 씻어 없앤다. 그것은 심지어 많은 세균을 죽이기도 한다. 그러나 당신이 잠을 자는 동안 당신의 입은 보다 적은 침을 만든다. **(A)** 이것은 당신 입속의 세균에게는 좋은 소식이다. 당신이 매일 밤 잠자리에 들면 당신의 입속의 세균은 (음식을) 먹기 위해 깨어 있는다! **(C)** 밤새도록 수백만의 세균이 죽어 냄새를 풍기기 시작한다. 그 결과는 아침의 입 냄새이다. 빨리 당신의 칫솔을 찾아라!

어휘

taste ⑲맛, 입맛　stay ⑧머물다; *～인 채로 있다　awake ⑲깨어 있는　have to do with ～와 관계가 있다　overnight ⑨밤새도록　result ⑲결과　toothbrush ⑲칫솔

구문 해설

1행 Many people wake up **with a bad taste and smell in their mouth**.

· with + 목적어 + 전치사구: ～을 …한 상태로

Unit Review   p.35

A Reading 1 smelly, dead, regularly, water, sweet　Reading 2 bacteria

B **1** roommate　**2** breath　**3** awake　**4** cause　**5** result　**6** common

Reading 2 해석

침은 보통 냄새 나는 입속의 세균들을 씻어 없애지만, 밤사이에 그 세균들은 죽어서 당신의 입에서 나쁜 냄새가 나게 만든다.

15

UNIT 08 Sports

Before Reading It's because people can enjoy golf in a large and wide field.

1 ④   **2** ①   **3** ③   **4** ②   **5** ③   **6** (1) T (2) F

해석

골프는 수백 년간 행해져 왔다. 그러나 누가 그것을 발명했는지 아무도 확실히 알지 못한다. 대부분의 사람들은 그것이 12세기에 스코틀랜드에서 시작되었다고 생각한다. 그 당시 양치기들은 그들의 양을 지키는 동안 종종 지루해졌다. 그래서 그들은 게임을 하나 발명했는데, 그것은 막대기로 토끼 굴에 돌을 밀어 넣는 것이었다. 이 게임은 곧 전국 곳곳에서 인기를 얻게 되었다. 스코틀랜드의 왕조차도 그것을 즐기기 시작했다! 17세기에 골프는 프랑스, 독일, 영국 같은 다른 나라들에 소개되었다.

오늘날에는 전 세계에 골프장이 있다. 그리고 6,000만 명 이상의 사람들이 그것을 즐긴다. 그러나 왜 그것이 그렇게 인기가 있는 것일까? 첫째, 골퍼들은 자연의 아름다움과 신선한 공기를 즐길 수 있다. 이것은 복잡한 도시에 사는 사람들에게는 큰 휴식이 된다. 둘째, 그것은 훌륭한 운동이다. 일반적으로 골프장은 매우 길어서 골퍼들은 많이 걸어야 한다. 골프채를 휘두르는 것 또한 골퍼의 상체를 강하게 해준다.

어휘

invent ⑧발명하다   century ⑲세기(100년)   shepherd ⑲양치기   push ⑧밀다   hole ⑲구멍, 굴   stick ⑲막대기 throughout ⑳~의 도처에   introduce ⑧소개하다   such as ~와 같은   nowadays ⑨오늘날   golf course 골프장 natural ⑲자연의   relaxing ⑲편안한   crowded ⑲붐비는, 복잡한   swing ⑧흔들다, 휘두르다   club ⑲(골프·하키 등의) 채   upper ⑲위쪽의   [문제] explain ⑧설명하다   suggest ⑧제안하다   clear ⑲명백한   tiring ⑲피곤하게 하는, 힘든 exercise ⑲운동

구문 해설

1행   **Golf has been played** *for* hundreds of years.
- has been played: 현재완료 수동태로 '(과거부터 지금까지) 행해져 왔다'는 계속의 의미
- for: ~ 동안

1행   But no one is sure **who invented it**.
- who invented it: '누가 그것을 발명했는지'의 의미의 간접의문문으로 여기서는 who가 의문사이자 주어 역할

3행   Back then, shepherds often became bored **while (they were) watching** their sheep.
- 접속사 while 뒤에는 '주어 + be동사'가 생략됨

16

②

해석

당신은 골프공이 무엇으로 만들어져 있다고 생각하는가? 최초의 골프공은 나무로 만들어졌다. 그것들은 겨우 100미터 정도만 날아갈 수 있었다. 나중에 골퍼들은 닭의 깃털을 가죽으로 덮어 공을 만들었다. 이것들은 조금 더 멀리 날아갈 수 있었다. 19세기에 공장들은 골프공을 고무와 플라스틱으로 만들기 시작했다. 흥미롭게도, 골퍼들은 긁힌 공들이 더 멀리 날아가는 것을 발견했다. (하지만 그들이 골프공을 만드는 데는 30일까지 걸리기도 하였다.) 그래서 그들은 그 안에 작은 구멍들을 만들기 시작했다. 오늘날, 공장에서는 각 골프공에 수백 개의 움푹 팬 홈들이 만들어진다. 대부분의 골프공에는 약 250~450개의 홈들이 있으며 이 공들은 약 270미터를 날아갈 수 있다!

어휘

travel ⑧여행하다; *이동하다   feather ⑲깃털   leather ⑲가죽   farther ⑨더 멀리 (far의 비교급)   factory ⑲공장   rubber ⑲고무   scratch ⑧긁다   up to ~까지   dimple ⑲보조개; *움푹 들어간 곳

구문 해설

1행   What **do you think** golf balls are made of?
• do you think가 의문사가 있는 간접의문문을 목적어로 취할 때, 의문사는 문장의 맨 앞에 위치함

Unit Review p.39

A Reading 1 shepherds, spread, enjoyed, exercise   Reading 2 dimples

B **1** push **2** crowded **3** shepherd **4** scratch **5** relaxing **6** introduce

Reading 2 해석

과거에 많은 여러 가지의 골프공들이 만들어졌지만, 그 중 움푹 팬 홈들이 있는 공이 가장 멀리 날아간다.

Reading 1

Before Reading Last year, I visited an animal shelter and helped with cleaning the cages there.

1 ④　**2** ①, ②　**3** ③　**4** ③　**5** it can change other people's lives　**6** (1) T　(2) F

해석

우리는 모두 어디에도 집만 한 곳이 없다는 것을 안다. 그러나 슬프게도, 집이 없는 사람들이 많이 있다. '해비타트(Habitat for Humanity)'는 이런 가난한 사람들을 위해 집을 짓는다. 그것은 1976년에 시작된 자선 단체이다. 해비타트는 자원봉사자들을 이용하여, 전 세계에 새 집을 짓는다.

해비타트에는 2가지 중요한 규정이 있다. 첫째, 집들은 무료가 아니다. 집주인들은 그것들에 대해 돈을 지불해야 한다. 그 돈은 그다음에 해비타트가 다른 집들을 지을 때 사용된다. 물론 그 가격은 매우 저렴하다. 둘째, 집주인들은 자원봉사자들이 그들의 새 집을 짓는 것을 도와야 한다. 이 규정들에는 충분한 이유가 있다. 해비타트는 집주인들이 그들 자신의 집을 위해 돈을 내고 그 집을 (직접) 지을 때 즐거워하며 자랑스러워한다는 것을 안다.

새 집들에 대해 기뻐하는 사람들은 집주인들만이 아니다. 해비타트에서 일하는 자원봉사자들 또한 자랑스러움을 느낀다. 이것은 그들이 자신들의 일이 다른 사람들의 삶을 변화시킬 수 있다는 것을 알기 때문이다. 결국 해비타트 덕분에 모두의 삶이 더 좋아진다.

어휘

habitat 圐 (동물들의) 서식지; *거주지　humanity 圐 인류, 인간　charity 圐 자선 단체　volunteer 圐 자원하는 圐 자원봉사자　rule 圐 규칙　free 圐 자유로운; *무료의　homeowner 圐 집주인　price 圐 가격, 값　pleased 圐 즐거운　proud 圐 자랑스러워하는　in the end 결국　thanks to ~ 덕분에　[문제] lesson 圐 수업; *교훈　move 圐 움직이다; *이사하다　right 圐 올바른

구문 해설

3행　It is a charity [**which** started in 1976].

· which 이하는 a charity를 수식하는 주격 관계대명사절

9행　Second, the owners have to **help the volunteers build** their new homes.

· help + 목적어 + (to) 동사원형: ~가 …하는 것을 돕다

①

해석

자원봉사 휴가는 보통의 휴가와 다르다. 해변에서 그냥 시간을 보내는 대신 당신이 어떤 봉사활동을 하는 것이다. 이것은 당신이 여행을 하는 동안 다른 사람들을 돕는 것을 즐길 수 있다는 것을 의미한다. 많은 종류의 자원봉사 휴가가 있다. 그러므로 당신은 당신의 성격과 어울리는 것을 쉽게 찾을 수 있다. 만일 당신이 많은 에너지를 갖고 있다면, 가난한 사람들을 위해 집을 짓는 것을 돕기를 좋아할지도 모른다. 만일 아이들을 좋아한다면, 당신은 학교에서 가난한 아이들을 가르치거나 병원에서 아픈 아이들을 도울 수 있다. 자원봉사 휴가는 힘든 일일 수 있지만 다른 사람들을 돕는다는 느낌은 멋진 선물이다.

어휘

usual ⑱보통의, 통상의   spend ⑧(시간을) 보내다   while 쩹~하는 동안   match ⑧~와 어울리다   energy ⑲에너지, 기운

구문 해설

2행   This means (that) you can **enjoy helping** others while you travel.
- enjoy는 동명사를 목적어로 취함

4행   So you can easily find **one** [*to match* your personality].
- one: a volunteer vacation을 가리키는 대명사
- to match: one을 수식하는 형용사적 용법의 to부정사로 '~할, ~하는'의 의미

Unit Review p.43

A   Reading 1   poor, free, proud, volunteers

B   **1** habitat   **2** humanity   **3** volunteer   **4** charity   **5** proud   **6** rule

Reading 1 해석

해비타트는 자선 단체이다. 1976년부터, 그 자선 단체는 가난한 사람들을 위해 집을 지었다. 집은 무료가 아니지만, 비싸지 않다. 해비타트는 집주인들에게 그들의 새 집에 대한 비용을 지불하도록 요청한다. 그들은 또한 해비타트가 집을 짓는 것을 도와야 한다. 이에 대한 이유가 있다. 집이 완성되면, 집주인들은 자랑스러워한다. 집을 짓는 것을 돕는 자원봉사자들 또한 행복해한다. 해비타트는 모두를 기분 좋게 만든다!

Before Reading Sure, I read the book and saw the animation too!

1 ② **2** ④ **3** She had to stand in the corner. **4** ③ **5** ③ **6** (1) T (2) F

해석

어느 날 학교에서 다이애나가 새로운 남학생을 가리켰다. "쟤가 길버트 블라이스야. 사촌들을 방문하고 막 돌아왔어. 그는 잘생겼지! 하지만 심한 장난꾸러기이니까 조심해."

얼마 후 앤은 길버트가 다른 여학생의 머리를 그녀의 의자에 묶는 것을 보았다.

"저건 못된 짓이야!"라고 앤은 생각했다.

그다음에 길버트는 앤이 자신을 보게 하려고 애썼다. 그러나 앤은 창밖을 바라보고 있었다. 그녀는 자신이 아름다운 호수변을 산책하는 모습을 상상했다. 그 순간 길버트가 그녀의 머리를 뒤에서 잡아당겼다.

"네 머리는 당근과 같은 색깔이구나." 그는 웃어댔다. "당근! 당근!"

앤이 그녀의 자리에서 벌떡 일어났다. "넌 못되고 불쾌한 아이야." 그녀는 소리쳤다. 그러더니 "꽝!"하고 자신의 석판을 길버트의 머리에 내리쳐 깨뜨렸다. 교실에 있던 모든 학생들이 놀랐다. 그들의 선생님은 매우 화가 나셨다. 앤은 벌로 구석에 서 있어야 했다. 길버트는 그것이 모두 그의 잘못이라고 설명하려 애썼다. 그러나 그것은 선생님에게 중요하지 않았다.

수업이 끝난 후 길버트는 앤에게 미안하다고 말했다. 앤은 길버트를 쳐다보지 않았다. 그녀는 그의 말이 들리지 않는 것처럼 행동했다.

어휘

point to ~을 가리키다 cousin 명 사촌 brat 명 장난꾸러기 tie 동 매다 mean 형 비열한, 못된 picture 동 상상하다 take a walk 산책하다 moment 명 순간 hateful 형 미운 shout 동 소리치다 smack 명 찰싹하는 소리 mad 형 미친; *몹시 화가 난 punishment 명 벌 explain 동 설명하다 matter 동 중요하다 [문제] miss 동 그리워하다; *빠지다 play a trick on ~을 놀리다 fault 명 잘못 bother 동 괴롭히다 daydream 동 몽상하다 nickname 명 별명

구문 해설

4행   Soon, Anne **saw Gilbert *tie*** another girl's hair *to* her chair.

- 지각동사(see) + 목적어 + 동사원형: ~가 …하는 것을 보다
- tie A to B: A를 B에 묶다

7행   She **pictured herself taking** a walk by the beautiful lake.

- picture + 목적어 + v-ing: ~가 …하는 것을 상상하다

10행   "Your hair is **the same** color **as** carrots," he laughed.

- the same A as B: B와 같은 A

④

해석

'빨강 머리 앤(Anne of Green Gables)'의 작가 루시 모드 몽고메리는 1874년 캐나다에서 태어났다. 어머니의 사망 후 몽고메리는 아직 아기였을 때 그녀의 할머니 할아버지의 집에 보내졌다. 그곳에서의 어린 시절은 그녀에게 '빨강 머리 앤'에 대한 많은 아이디어를 주었다. 바깥에서 놀고 할아버지의 이야기를 들으면서 그녀의 상상력은 자라났다. 나중에 그녀는 선생님으로 일했으나 작가가 되기를 꿈꿨다. 그러나 그녀가 1905년에 등장인물인 앤을 만들었을 때, 출판사들은 관심을 보이지 않았다. 이것은 몽고메리를 실망시켜서 그녀는 그 이야기를 낡은 모자 상자에 치워 두었다. 그러나 수년 후에 그녀는 다시 시도했다. 그리고 1908년에, '빨강 머리 앤'이 마침내 출판되었다. 그 후, 몽고메리는 앤에 대한 여러 편의 인기 있는 이야기들을 더 썼다. 그 후 한 세기가 넘도록 그녀의 책들은 아직도 전 세계 사람들에게 감동을 주고 있다.

어휘

death ⑲사망   still ⑯여전히   childhood ⑲어린 시절   imagination ⑲상상력   outdoors ⑯야외에서   dream of v-ing ~하는 것을 꿈꾸다   character ⑲등장인물   publisher ⑲출판사[업자] (publish ⑧출판하다)   disappoint ⑧실망시키다   put away 치워두다   finally ⑯마침내   century ⑲세기   touch ⑧감동시키다   worldwide ⑯전 세계에 [문제] imaginative ⑲상상력이 풍부한   make up (이야기 등을) 지어[만들어] 내다

구문 해설

9행   Her imagination grew **as** she played outdoors and ... stories.
       • as: ~할 때, ~하면서

10행   Later, she ┌ worked **as** a teacher
                  │ but
                  └ dreamed of becoming a writer.
       • as: '~로서'라는 뜻의 전치사로 역할이나 자격을 나타냄

Unit Review   p.47

A   **Reading 1** handsome, mean, angry, fault   **Reading 2** writer

B   **1** publisher   **2** cousin   **3** mean   **4** explain   **5** character   **6** tie

Reading 1 해석

다이애나는 앤에게 학급에 새로 온 남학생인 길버트 블라이스에 대해 경고한다. 그는 잘생겼지만 장난이 심하다. 앤은 그가 다른 학생에게 장난을 치는 것을 보면서 그가 못된 아이라는 것을 알 수 있다. 앤이 쳐다보고 있지 않을 때 길버트는 그녀의 머리카락을 잡아당기고 빨간색 머리카락을 가지고 그녀를 놀린다. 앤은 너무 화가 나서 자신의 석판으로 그의 머리를 내리친다. 길버트가 그것은 그의 잘못이라고 말하지만, 선생님은 앤에게 구석에 가서 서 있으라고 말한다. 길버트는 사과하려고 하지만, 앤은 그에게 못 들은 척한다.

Reading 2 해석

성공적인 작가가 되려는 루시 모드 몽고메리의 꿈은 그녀의 등장인물 앤을 통해 이루어졌다.

UNIT 11 Culture

Reading 1

pp.48-49

Before Reading The sour and sweet fruit! They taste so good.

1 ② **2** ③ **3** the kiwi bird is New Zealand's national animal **4** ① **5** ③ **6** ④

해석

뉴질랜드는 키위로 유명하다. 그런데 키위는 정확히 무엇일까?

원래 키위는 갈색의 작은 새이다. 이 새는 뉴질랜드 태생이다. 키위 새는 둥근 몸통에 작은 날개와 짧은 깃털을 갖고 있다. 이것은 날지 못한다. 뉴질랜드에는 많은 키위 새가 있었다. 그러나 지금은 몇 천 마리만 남았다.

키위는 또한 뉴질랜드 출신의 사람을 칭하는 말이다. 그 이유는 키위 새가 뉴질랜드의 국조(국가를 상징하는 새)이기 때문이다. 그래서 뉴질랜드 사람들이 외국에 가면, 그들은 종종 '키위'라고 불린다.

당신은 아마도 마지막 종류의 키위를 이미 알고 있을 것인데, 바로 과일이다. 그러나 왜 그것이 키위라고 불리는지 짐작할 수 있는가? 그것은 그 과일이 뉴질랜드에서 재배되며 키위 새처럼 생겼기 때문이다. 그것은 키위 새처럼 작고 둥글며 짧은 갈색 털로 덮여 있다. 그러나 뉴질랜드에서 이것은 '키위'가 아닌 '키위프룻(kiwifruit)'이라고 불린다. 그런 식으로 사람들은 새와 사람들과 과일을 헷갈리지 않는다!

어휘

be famous for ~로 유명하다 exactly 부 정확히 original 형 원래의 native 형 *태생의; 원주민의 round 형 둥근 leave 동 떠나다; *남기다 national 형 국가의 overseas 부 해외로 probably 부 아마도 grow 동 자라다; 재배하다, 기르다 look like ~처럼 보이다 cover 동 덮다 that way 그런 식으로 [문제] natural 형 자연의 beauty 명 미, 아름다움 curious 형 호기심이 많은 confused 형 혼란스러운, 헷갈리는 weird 형 기이한, 이상한 related 형 관련된

구문 해설

5행 There **used to be** a lot of kiwis in New Zealand.

- used to + 동사원형: ~이었다, ~했었다 (과거의 습관이나 상태를 표현)

11행 You probably already know the last kind of kiwi — **the fruit**.

- 대시(–) 이하는 the last kind of kiwi에 대한 구체적 예임

12행 But can you guess **why it's called a kiwi**?

- why 이하는 '의문사 + 주어 + 동사'의 간접의문문으로, guess의 목적어 역할을 함

Reading 2 p.50

③

해석

뉴질랜드를 생각하면 언제나 뉴질랜드 원주민인 마오리족이 생각난다. 그들은 1,000년 전에 폴리네시아에서 그곳으로 배를 타고 갔으며, 전국 각지에서 작은 집단들을 이루어 살기 시작했다. **(B)** 각 집단은 그들만의 역사와 문화를 발전시켰다. 19세기에 영국인들이 뉴질랜드에 도착했다. 그들은 뉴질랜드를 통치하기를 원했고, 그래서 마오리 족장들과 협정을 맺었다. **(C)** 그들은 마오리족의 생활 방식을 보호해 주기로 약속했다. 그러나, 오랜 세월 동안 마오리족은 어려운 시기를 보냈다. 그들은 질병과 영국인들과의 전쟁으로 죽었다. 그들은 전쟁에서 그들의 토지의 대부분도 잃었다. **(A)** 하지만 마오리족은 살아남았다. 오늘날 뉴질랜드에는 87만 5000명 이상의 마오리족들이 있고 그들의 문화와 언어는 여전히 중요하다.

어휘

sail ⑧ 항해하다   survive ⑧ 살아남다   culture ⑲ 문화   language ⑲ 언어   develop ⑧ 발달시키다   control
⑧ 지배하다   agreement ⑲ 일치; *협정   leader ⑲ 지도자   protect ⑧ 보호하다   a way of life 생활 방식   though
⑨ 그러나   disease ⑲ 질병   as well ~도 역시

구문 해설

1행 We **cannot** think of New Zealand **without thinking** of the Maori, the native people of New
Zealand.
=

- cannot ~ without v-ing: …하지 않고는 ~할 수가 없다, ~하면 언제나 …하다

Unit Review p.51

A [Reading 1] flightless, person, brown, kiwifruit [Reading 2] survive

B **1** cover **2** sail **3** overseas **4** agreement **5** native **6** protect

Reading 2 해석

비록 영국이 뉴질랜드를 통치하기 위해 싸웠지만, 마오리족 원주민과 그들의 문화 및 언어는 오늘날에도 여전히 살아있다.

pp.52-53

Reading 1

Before Reading No, I can't give up my favorite foods like hamburgers and fried chicken!

1 ②　　**2** ③　　**3** often have a hard time getting them　　**4** ①　　**5** ②　　**6** ③

해석

완전 채식주의 식단은 건강을 증진시키는 것으로 최근 인기를 끌고 있다. 하지만 당신은 완전 채식주의 식단을 시도하기 전에 이 식단의 이점들과 문제점들에 대해 생각해야 한다.

루카: 완전 채식주의 식단에는 많은 건강상의 이점이 있습니다. 식물성 식품은 많은 심각한 질병들의 위험을 줄여줍니다. 연구원들은 심지어 완전 채식주의자들이 체중과 심장 문제의 위험이 더 낮다는 것을 발견했습니다.

메이브: 완전 채식주의자들은 종종 비타민 D와 B12를 얻는 데 어려움을 겪습니다. 식물성 식품은 또한 충분한 칼슘이나 철분을 제공하지 않습니다. 이것은 대부분 고기에서 발견됩니다.

노바: 소 농장은 많은 양의 온실가스를 생산함으로써 환경을 해칩니다. 하지만, 식물은 많은 온실가스를 생산하지 않습니다. 그래서 완전 채식주의 식단은 지구 온난화에 맞서 싸우는 것을 도울 수 있습니다.

핀: 완전 채식주의자가 되기 위해서는 매우 부지런해야 합니다. 왜냐하면 여러분은 항상 식품의 라벨을 읽어야 하기 때문입니다. (이 라벨들은 우리에게 식품에 대한 정보를 알려주어야 합니다.) 만약 그렇게 하지 않는다면, 여러분은 필수적인 비타민과 미네랄을 얻을 수 없을 것입니다. 여러분은 또한 비타민과 미네랄이 들어있는 알약을 먹어야 할 수도 있습니다.

어휘

vegan 몡 톙 완전 채식주의자(의)　　diet 몡 식단　　popular 톙 인기 있는　　recently 뷔 최근에　　improve 톰 개선하다. 향상시키다　　health 몡 건강　　benefit 몡 혜택, 이득　　decrease 톰 감소시키다　　risk 몡 위험　　serious 톙 심각한　　researcher 몡 연구원　　low 톙 낮은 (비교급 lower)　　weight 몡 몸무게　　offer 톰 제공하다　　iron 몡 철분　　meat 몡 고기　　farm 몡 농장　　environment 몡 환경　　produce 톰 생산하다　　amount 몡 양　　greenhouse gas 온실가스　　global warming 지구 온난화　　diligent 톙 부지런한　　label 몡 표, 라벨, 상표　　all the time 항상　　information 몡 정보　　necessary 톙 필수적인　　pill 몡 알약　　[문제] calorie 몡 열량　　loss 몡 손실; 줄임, 감량　　lower 톰 낮추다, 내리다　　impact 몡 영향

구문 해설

1행　　Vegan diets **have become** popular recently for *improving one's health.*
- have become: '~해 오고 있다'의 의미로 계속을 나타내는 현재완료
- improving one's health: 전치사 for의 목적어로 쓰인 동명사구

9행　　Vegans often **have a hard time getting** vitamins D and B12.
- have a hard time v-ing: ~하는 데 어려움을 겪다

14행   So a vegan diet can **help fight** against global warming.

       • help + (to) 동사원형: ~하도록 돕다, ~에 도움이 되다

Reading 2   p.54

④

해석

당신은 완전 채식주의 식단을 시작하고 싶지만 당신이 가장 좋아하는 음식 중 몇몇을 포기하는 것에 대해 걱정하고 있는가? 음, 걱정하지 마라! 종종 진짜 고기처럼 맛이 나고 심지어 그렇게 보이는 고기가 아닌 음식들이 있다! 두유로 만든 부드러운 음식인 두부는 고기가 아닌 음식 중 하나이다. 그것은 많은 기본 단백질을 포함하고 있다. 그래서 당신은 계란 대신 두부를 먹으면 된다. 버섯, 렌즈콩, 병아리콩과 같은 특정 채소도 당신이 먹는 고기를 대체할 수 있다. 이 채소들이 식물성 기름이나 밀 글루텐과 섞일 때, 그것들은 고기와 같은 음식으로 바뀔 수 있다. 당신은 가장 좋아하는 음식을 채소로 대신해서 즐길 수 있다! 그러니 한 번 시도해 보는 게 어떤가?

어휘

give up 포기하다   favorite 혱 가장 좋아하는   taste 동 맛이 ~하다, ~ 맛이 나다   soy milk 두유   type 명 종류   contain 동 포함하다   protein 명 단백질   instead of ~ 대신에   certain 혱 어떤   vegetable 명 채소   mushroom 명 버섯   replace 동 대체하다   give it a try 시도하다, 한번 해보다   [문제] wheat 명 밀

구문 해설

1행   Do you want **to start** a vegan diet but you're worried about *giving up some of your favorite foods*?

       • to start: '~하는 것'의 의미로 want의 목적어로 사용된 명사적 용법의 to부정사

       • giving up 이하는 '~하는 것'의 의미로 전치사 about의 목적어로 사용된 동명사구

2행   There are <u>non-meat foods</u> [**that** often taste and even look like real meat]!

       • that 이하는 non-meat foods를 수식하는 주격 관계대명사절

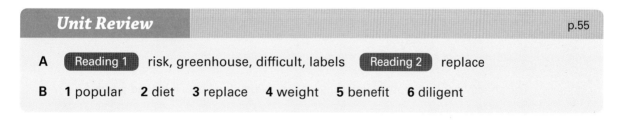

Unit Review   p.55

A   Reading 1   risk, greenhouse, difficult, labels   Reading 2   replace

B   **1** popular   **2** diet   **3** replace   **4** weight   **5** benefit   **6** diligent

Reading 2 해석

두부와 특정 채소와 같은 음식들은 고기를 <u>대체하는</u> 데 사용될 수 있다.

Reading 1 pp.56-57

Before Reading He was a US president. I read stories about him.

1 ③　**2** ②　**3** ②　**4** ②　**5** ①　**6** (1) F　(2) F

해석

에이브러햄 링컨은 유명한 미국 대통령이었다. 그런데 왜 그가 당선되었을까? 어떤 사람들은 그가 매우 훌륭한 정치인이었기 때문이었다고 말한다. 다른 사람들은 그가 매우 똑똑했기 때문이었다고 말한다. 그러나 어쩌면 다른 이유가 있을지도 모른다. 그것은 그가 11살짜리 소녀에게서 받은 충고일 수도 있다!

1860년에 링컨은 대통령에 출마하고 있었다. 그레이스 베델이라는 이름의 소녀는 링컨의 신념을 좋아했다. 그녀는 그가 이기기를 원했다. 어느 날, 그녀는 링컨의 사진을 보고 있었다. 그녀의 방에 든 그림자가 그의 마른 얼굴의 일부를 덮었고 그것은 보기 좋았다. 그래서 그녀는 링컨에게 충고의 편지를 쓰기로 결심했다. 그녀는 그의 마른 얼굴이 우스꽝스러워 보이지만 턱수염이 있으면 더 좋아 보일 거라고 말했다. 그러면 사람들이 그를 더 좋아할 테니 말이다.

그다음엔 어떻게 되었을까? 링컨은 턱수염을 길렀고, 이후 그 해에 그는 대통령으로 당선되었다! 머지않아 그는 그레이스의 마을을 방문했다. (그는 기차로 이동하는 것을 좋아했다.) 그는 그에게 그토록 특별한 충고를 해준 소녀를 만나고 싶었다. 마을의 모든 사람들이 대통령의 방문에 놀랐다. 그들은 한 어린 소녀가 역사를 바꿀 수 있으리라곤 전혀 알지 못했다!

어휘

president 명 대통령　politician 명 정치인　intelligent 형 똑똑한, 지성을 갖춘　advice 명 충고　run for ~에 출마하다　win 동 이기다　shadow 명 그림자　skinny 형 깡마른　beard 명 턱수염　grow 동 (수염·손톱 등을) 기르다　elect 동 선출하다　before long 머지 않아　have no idea 전혀 모르다　[문제] by mistake 실수로　relationship 명 관계　slim 형 날씬한 (비교급 slimmer)　freedom 명 자유　upset 동 화나게 하다　in the end 결국

구문 해설

4행　It could be the advice [(that) he got from an eleven-year-old girl]!

・he 앞에는 목적격 관계대명사 which 또는 that이 생략되어 있음

8행　The shadows in her room covered part of his skinny face, and it **looked good**.

・look + 형용사: ~해 보이다

15행　He wanted to meet the girl [who **had given** him such special advice].

・had given: 주절의 과거 시제보다 앞선 때의 내용을 가리키는 과거완료 시제

⑤

해석

에이브러햄 링컨이 젊은 청년이었을 때, 그는 '정직한 에이브'라는 별명을 얻었다. 그는 한 상점에서 일하면서 그의 성격으로 유명해졌다. 어느 날 저녁, 상점의 돈을 세던 중 링컨은 자신이 몇 센트를 더 많이 갖고 있다는 것을 발견했다. 그는 자신이 어느 고객에게 잔돈을 너무 적게 주었다는 것을 알아냈다. 그날 밤, 그는 그 고객에게 돈을 돌려주기 위해 수 마일을 걸어갔다. 또 한 번은, 링컨은 자신이 어느 여인에게 그녀의 돈에 비해 너무 적은 차를 주었다고 생각했다. 그래서 그는 차를 조금 더 가지고 그녀의 집으로 갔다. 나중에 링컨은 미국의 대통령이 되었고 그는 평생 동안 거짓말을 한 번도 하지 않은 것으로 전해진다.

어휘

honest ⑧정직한 (honesty ⑲정직) well-known for ~으로 잘 알려진 personality ⑲성격 count ⑧(수를) 세다
customer ⑲고객 change ⑲잔돈 return ⑧돌려주다 carry ⑧들고 가다 lie ⑲거짓말 [문제] fortune ⑲행운
earn ⑧(돈을) 벌다; *얻다 overcome ⑧극복하다 truthful ⑧정직한 bring about ~을 일으키다, 생기게 하다

구문 해설

13행 ..., and **it is said that** he never told a lie in his life.
· it is said that ~: ~이라고들 말한다, ~이라고 전해진다

Unit Review p.59

A [Reading 1] skinny, beard, advice, helped [Reading 2] personality
B **1** return **2** politician **3** lie **4** change **5** skinny **6** elect

Reading 1 해석

1860년에, 에이브러햄 링컨은 미국의 대통령이 되려고 노력 중이었다. 11살짜리 한 소녀는 그의 사진을 보고 그의 마른 얼굴이 우스꽝스러워 보인다고 생각했다. 그녀는 그가 턱수염이 있으면 훨씬 더 좋아 보일 거라고 생각했다. 그래서 그녀는 그에게 편지 한 통을 보냈고 그가 턱수염을 길러야 한다고 제안했다. 그는 그녀의 충고를 받아들였고 곧 대통령에 당선됐다! 나중에, 그는 자신을 아주 많이 도와주었던 그 어린 소녀를 만나기 위해 그녀의 마을을 방문했다.

Reading 2 해석

에이브러햄 링컨은 상점 직원과 대통령으로서 일하면서 그의 성격에 대한 유명한 이야기들로 인해 '정직한 에이브'로 알려져 있다.

Reading 1   pp.60-61

Before Reading   We use metal coins. They are all round but different in size.

1 ③   **2** ②   **3** pick up and hold them without worrying about sharp corners   **4** ④
5 ③   **6** ③

해석

여러분은 주머니에 동전이 있는가? 하나 꺼내서 그것을 자세히 보아라. 그것은 동그랗지 않은가? 여러분은 왜 대부분의 동전이 둥근지 알고 있는가? 여기에 그 이유가 있다.

우선, 그것들은 일상생활에서 사용하기 쉽다. 여러분은 날카로운 모서리에 대해서 걱정하지 않고 둥근 동전을 집어서 쥐고 있을 수 있다. 모서리가 없기 때문에, 동전은 안전하고 사람들을 다치게 할 수 없다. 게다가, 그것들은 기계와 잘 작동한다. (기계들은 정기적으로 교체되어야 한다.) 둥근 동전은 굴러갈 수 있기 때문에, 자판기와 동전 분류기에서 쉽게 움직여질 수 있다. 이것은 그것들이 기계 안에서 걸려 있지 않을 것이라는 것을 의미한다. 게다가, 그것들은 닳을 가능성이 낮다. 동전은 오랫동안 지속되도록 만들어진다. 모서리들은 자주 물건들에 닿기 때문에, 그것들은 더 빨리 닳는다. 하지만 둥근 동전은 이런 문제가 없다. 마지막으로, 둥근 모양은 공장에서 쉽게 생산된다. 원은 다른 모양보다 더 단순해서, 그것들은 만들기에 더 빠르다. 그러므로 공장들은 많은 둥근 동전을 동시에 만들 수 있다.

어휘

coin 몡동전   pocket 몡주머니   closely 뷔자세히   first of all 우선   sharp 혱뾰족한   corner 몡모서리   hurt 됭다치게 하다   in addition 게다가   regularly 뷔정기[규칙]적으로   roll 됭굴러가다   vending machine 자판기   sort 됭분류하다, 구분하다   get stuck 꼼짝 못하게 되다   wear down 닳다, 마모되다   last 됭오래가다, 지속되다   rub 됭문지르다   shape 몡모양   at the same time 동시에   [문제] invent 됭발명하다   hardly 뷔거의 ~않는   function 됭기능하다

구문 해설

2행   Do you know **why most coins are round**?
       • why 이하는 know의 목적어 역할을 하는 간접의문문으로 '의문사 + 주어 + 동사'의 어순을 취함

11행   Furthermore, they **are** less **likely to wear** down.
       • be likely to-v: ~하기 쉽다, ~할 가능성이 있다

14행   Circles are simpler than other shapes, so they're faster [**to make**].

       • to make: '~하기에'의 의미로 형용사 faster를 수식하는 부사적 용법의 to부정사

①

해석

요즘, 사람들은 물건을 사기 위해 종종 신용 카드나 직불 카드를 사용한다. 하지만 현금도 사용해야 하는 몇 가지 훌륭한 이유들이 있다. 우선, 현금은 모든 판매자들이 받는다. 사업체들은 신용 카드나 직불 카드로 결제하기 위한 특별한 기기가 필요하다. 그래서, 몇몇 작은 가게들과 식당들은 현금만 받는다. 게다가, 현금을 사용하는 것은 여러분이 돈을 덜 쓰도록 도울 수 있다. 카드로 결제할 때는 돈을 더 쓰는 게 일반적이다. 하지만 현금으로 결제하면, 여러분이 얼마나 많은 돈을 가지고 있는지 알 수 있다. 그래서 많은 돈을 쓰는 것이 더 어렵다. 돈으로 지불하는 것은 판매자와 구매자 모두에게 좋다!

어휘

credit card 신용 카드   debit card 직불 카드   reason 뗑 이유   cash 뗑 현금   accept 뚱 받아들이다   seller 뗑 판매자
device 뗑 기구   payment 뗑 지불 (pay 뚱 지불하다)   common 혱 흔한   spend 뚱 (돈을) 쓰다   buyer 뗑 구매자
[문제] discount 뗑 할인

구문 해설

1행   These days, people often use their credit or debit card **to buy** things.
- to buy: '~하기 위하여'의 의미로 목적을 나타내는 부사적 용법의 to부정사

5행   **When (you are) paying** with a card, *it's* common *to spend* more money.
- 접속사 when 뒤에는 '주어 + be동사'가 생략됨
- it은 가주어이고, to spend는 진주어로 '~하는 것'의 의미

Unit Review p.63

A Reading 1 round, machines, wear down, make   Reading 2 spending
B **1** discount **2** invent **3** sharp **4** reason **5** sort **6** roll

Reading 2 해석

현금으로 쇼핑하는 것은 좋을 수 있는데, 왜냐하면 모든 판매자들이 그것을 받고, 그것을 사용하면 당신이 돈을 너무 많이 쓰는 것을 막을 수 있기 때문이다.

Reading 1   pp.64-65

Before Reading   I went to the Carnival of Venice in Italy. It was amazing.

1 ③   **2** early October for nine days   **3** ②   **4** ③   **5** ③   **6** ④

해석

'높이, 높이, 저 멀리, 내 아름답고 내 아름다운 열기구야!'라는 노래 가사는 앨버커키 국제 열기구 축제에 있는 사람들이 공중에 떠 있는 경이로운 물건(열기구)에 대해 어떻게 느끼는지를 묘사한다. 미국 뉴멕시코에서 열리는 이것은 세계 최대의 열기구 축제이다. 10월 초 9일 동안, 이 축제는 전 세계에서 온 방문객들에게 잊을 수 없는 경험을 제공한다.

가장 인기 있는 행사는 모든 열기구들이 이륙하는 것을 보는 것이다. 색색의 커다란 풍선을 단 700개의 바구니를 상상해 보라. 그런 다음 마치 오케스트라처럼 다 함께, 버너가 큰 소리를 내고 그것들 모두가 떠오른다. 당신을 놀라게 하기에 충분하지 않다고? 그렇다면 열기구 불빛의 밤(Evening Balloon Glow)에 가보아라. 빛나는 열기구들은 마치 저녁 하늘을 날아다니는 반딧불이처럼 보인다. 그밖에 이 아름다운 것들이 할 수 있는 것은 무엇일까? 그것들은 어떤 것이 가장 멀리 날아갈 수 있는지 가리기 위해 경주를 할 수 있다.

열기구 쇼들 외에 즐길 수 있는 많은 다른 행사들이 있다. 당신은 라이브 음악을 듣고 열기구 발견 센터(Balloon Discovery Center)를 방문할 수도 있다. (열기구의 역사는 그리 오래되지 않았다.) 그리고 만일 당신이 정말로 높이 높이 저 멀리 날아가고 싶다면 열기구를 타 보라!

어휘

balloon 몡풍선; *기구 (hot air balloon 열기구)   describe 통묘사하다   fiesta 몡축제 (= festival)   floating 혱떠있는   wonder 몡*놀라운 물건; 경이   unforgettable 혱잊을 수 없는   lift off 이륙하다   burner 몡버너   roar 통큰 소리를 내다   rise 통솟아오르다   take one's breath away ~을 놀라게 하다   glow 몡(불꽃 없이 타는 물체의) 빛 통빛나다   firefly 몡반딧불이   farthest 뷘가장 멀리 (far의 최상급)   in addition to ~ 외에도   discovery 몡발견   ride 몡타고가기 통타다   [문제] tourist 몡여행자, 관광객   site 몡장소   fill 통가득 차다, 채우다   advise 통조언[충고]하다   take a deep breath 심호흡하다

구문 해설

8행   The most popular event is **watching** all the balloons lift off.

• watching: be동사의 보어로 사용된 동명사로 '~하는 것'의 의미

• 지각동사(watch) + 목적어 + 동사원형: ~가 …하는 것을 보다

13행   They can race **to see** which can travel the farthest.

• to see: '~하기 위하여'의 의미로 목적을 나타내는 부사적 용법의 to부정사

• which 이하는 see의 목적어로 쓰인 간접의문문

16행   And if you really **do** want to go up, up and away, take a balloon ride!

• do: 동사 want를 강조하는 조동사

⑤

해석

여러분은 풍선을 타고 공중을 날고 싶은가? 그렇다면 터키의 카파도키아를 방문하라! 그곳은 열기구를 타기에 아주 좋은 곳이다. **(C)** 한 가지 이유는 날씨가 아주 좋기 때문이다. 열기구는 날기 위해 잔잔한 날씨를 필요로 하고, 카파도키아는 거의 일 년 내내 (날씨가) 좋다. 사실, 그곳에서 열기구는 매년 약 250일을 날 수 있다! **(B)** 훌륭한 날씨 외에도, 카파도키아는 열기구를 위한 많은 개방된 공간도 가지고 있다. 탐험할 많은 장소들이 있고, 야생동물은 없다. 그러므로, 그 열기구들은 하늘 높이 또는 땅 가까이 날 수 있다. **(A)** 하지만 카파도키아에서 풍선을 타는 가장 좋은 이유는 풍경 때문이다. 그곳은 아름다운 계곡, 어두운 동굴, 그리고 숨겨진 도시들로 가득하다. 매년 수천 명의 관광객들이 카파도키아로 가는 것은 당연하다!

어휘

air 명공기; *공중, 허공   visit 동방문하다   amazing 형놀라운   landscape 명풍경   be full of ~로 가득 차다   valley 명계곡   cave 명동굴   hidden 형숨겨진   no wonder 당연히 ~하다   thousands of 수천의 ~   weather 명날씨   space 명공간   explore 동탐험하다   wildlife 명야생동물   excellent 형훌륭한, 탁월한   calm 형침착한, 차분한; *잔잔한

구문 해설

3행   But the best reason [**to ride** a balloon in Cappadocia] is the landscape.
　　　　　　주어 ▲ ＿＿＿＿＿＿＿＿＿＿＿　　　　　　　　　　　　　동사

　　　　• to ride: the best reason을 수식하는 형용사적 용법의 to부정사로 '~하는'의 의미

Unit Review p.67

A   **Reading 1** largest, held, rise up, glowing   **Reading 2** landscape
B   **1** landscape   **2** wildlife   **3** glow   **4** discovery   **5** tourist   **6** weather

Reading 1 해석

앨버커키 국제 열기구 축제는 세계에서 가장 큰 열기구 축제이다. 그 축제는 미국의 뉴멕시코에서 10월마다 9일 동안 열린다. 수백 개의 열기구들이 모두 함께 떠올라서, 하늘을 그것들의 아름다운 색으로 가득 채운다. 또한 저녁에 열기구 행사가 있는데, 빛나는 열기구들이 밤하늘에 떠다닌다. 그리고 열기구 경주도 있다. 열기구 쇼 외에도, 사람들이 이 멋진 축제에서 즐길 만한 재미있는 활동들이 많이 있다.

Reading 2 해석

터키의 카파도키아는 잔잔한 날씨, 많은 공간, 그리고 놀라운 풍경을 가지고 있기 때문에 열기구를 타기에 좋은 장소이다.

Reading 1   pp.68-69

Before Reading I use my personal cup instead of paper cups. Also, I try to recycle things.

1 ① **2** ② **3** ④ **4** ② **5** ① **6** ④

해석

3월의 마지막 토요일에 이상한 일이 발생한다. 전 세계의 도시에서 한 시간 동안 전등이 꺼진다! 그러나 그것은 사고가 아니다. 그것은 지구촌 전등 끄기(Earth Hour)라고 불리는 행사이다.

지구촌 전등 끄기는 2007년에 시작되었다. 그것은 세계자연기금(WWF)에 의해 계획되었다. 세계자연기금은 환경을 보호하기 위해 노력하는 단체이다. 그들은 사람들에게 한 시간 동안 전등을 꺼 달라고 요청했다. (전등 없이 하루를 보내는 것은 우리가 생각하는 것만큼 쉽지 않다.) 더 적은 불빛은 더 적은 에너지가 사용됨을 의미한다. 그리고 더 적은 에너지를 사용하는 것은 더 적은 오염이 발생되는 것을 의미한다. 첫 번째 지구촌 전등 끄기는 대성공이었고, 이제는 매년 한 번씩 열리고 있다.

어떤 사람들은 지구촌 전등 끄기가 어리석다고 생각한다. 그들은 한 시간은 변화를 가져올 만큼 충분히 길지 않다고 말한다. 물론 그들이 옳다. 그러나 지구촌 전등 끄기는 하나의 상징이다. 그것은 사람들에게 에너지를 절약하는 것이 중요하다는 것을 보여 준다. 그것은 또한 협동을 통해 그들이 변화를 가져올 수 있다는 것을 보여 준다. 한 사람의 작은 선택들이 전 세계적으로 커다란 영향을 미칠 수 있다.

어휘

go out (불 등이) 꺼지다   accident 똉 사고; 우연 (by accident 우연히)   event 똉 행사   earth 똉 지구   plan 똉 계획하다
fund 똉 기금   protect 똉 보호하다   turn off (불 등을) 끄다   pollution 똉 오염   success 똉 성공   silly 똉 어리석은
make a difference 변화를 가져오다, 차이가 있다   save 똉 절약하다   choice 똉 선택   have an effect 영향을 미치다
throughout 쩐 ～의 도처에   [문제] wild 똉 야생   promise 똉 약속   symbol 똉 상징   uncomfortable 똉 불편한
drop 똉 물방울   ocean 똉 바다

구문 해설

1행   On the last Saturday of March, **something strange** happens.
       • something과 같이 -thing으로 끝나는 대명사는 형용사가 그 뒤에서 수식함

9행   **Fewer** lights mean (that) *less* energy is used.
       • fewer: few의 비교급으로 '(수가) 더 적은'의 의미
       • less: little의 비교급으로 '(양이) 더 적은'의 의미
       • less 이하는 mean의 목적어로 앞에 접속사 that이 생략되어 있음

13행   They say (that) one hour isn't **long enough to make** a difference.
       • 형용사 + enough to-v: ～할 만큼 충분히 …한
       • one hour 이하는 say의 목적어로 앞에 접속사 that이 생략되어 있음

②

해석

세계자연기금(WWF)은 환경을 위해 일하는 단체이다. 그것은 1961년에 스위스에서 시작되었고 현재는 100개 이상의 나라에 5백만 명 이상의 회원들이 있다. 세계자연기금의 목표는 환경 훼손을 막고, 모든 식물과 동물을 보호하는 것이다. 이를 위해 그 단체는 자연환경을 보호해서 동물들이 그곳에서 계속 살 수 있도록 한다. 그것은 또한 정부가 사냥꾼들과 다른 위험들로부터 동물들을 보호하도록 장려하기도 한다. 가장 중요한 것으로, 세계자연기금은 전 세계 사람들에게 미래를 위해 지구를 깨끗하고 아름답게 유지하라고 가르친다.

어휘

Switzerland 똉스위스   goal 똉목표   damage 똉손상   natural 휑자연의   continue 똥계속하다   encourage 똥장려하다   government 똉정부   hunter 똉사냥꾼   [문제] guard 똥지키다, 보호하다

구문 해설

4행   **To do so,** it protects natural places *so that* animals *can* continue to live there.
· do so는 앞 문장에 나온 내용(stop damage ... animals)을 가리킴
· so that ~ can ...: ~가 …할 수 있도록

7행   Most importantly, the WWF **teaches people around the world to** *keep* the earth clean and *beautiful* for the future.
· teach + 목적어 + to-v: ~에게 …하라고 가르치다
· keep + 목적어 + 형용사: ~을 …하게 유지[보존]하다

Unit Review   p.71

A   Reading 1   held, turn off, symbol, together

B   **1** throughout   **2** goal   **3** encourage   **4** save   **5** choice   **6** pollution

Before Reading They do research about space, develop spaceships, and train astronauts.

1 ④ **2** ② **3** ② **4** any dangerous gases in the space station **5** ① **6** (1) F (2) T (3) T

해석

연기 탐지기, MRI, 그리고 운동화. 이 모든 발명품들은 어떤 공통점이 있을까? 이상하게 들릴지도 모르지만 그것들은 모두 우주 연구에 의해 가능해졌다.

나사(NASA)는 그들의 우주 프로그램을 위한 새로운 과학 기술들과 제품들을 만들기 위해 연구를 한다. 그러나 이 연구는 또한 우리가 지구에서 사용할 수 있는 제품들도 만든다. 한 가지 예는 연기 탐지기이다. 그것은 1973년 우주 정거장에서 위험한 가스를 탐지하는 데 처음 사용되었다. 현재 연기 탐지기는 대부분의 집과 건물에서 사람들에게 불이 났음을 경고하는 데 사용된다. 나사는 또한 우주선으로부터 보내진 신호를 더 명확하게 만드는 방법을 개발했다. 이 기술 덕분에 의사들은 현재 MRI를 가지고 있다. 또한, 운동화를 위한 재료도 우주 비행사들을 위한 특수 장화에서 생겨났다. 그것은 달릴 때 생기는 충격을 줄여 준다.

어떤 사람들은 나사가 그것의 우주 연구에 너무 많은 돈을 쓴다고 말한다. 그리고 그것의 연구에 매년 수십억 달러의 비용이 드는 것은 사실이다. 그러나 나사의 연구는 단지 우주에만 머물러 있지 않다. 지구에 있는 사람들도 때로는 매일 그것을 사용하게 된다.

어휘

smoke 몡연기   detector 몡탐지기 (detect 동탐지하다)   invention 몡발명품   have in common 공통점이 있다
(common 혱보통의, 평범한)   space 몡우주   research 몡연구, 조사   product 몡제품   space station 우주 정거장
warn 동경고하다   signal 몡신호   spacecraft 몡우주선 (= spaceship)   material 몡재료, 물질   astronaut 몡우주
비행사   lessen 동줄이다   shock 몡충격   cost 동~의 비용이 들다   get to-v ~하게 되다   [문제] daily 혱매일의
competition 몡경쟁   cure 동치료하다   serious 혱심각한   illness 몡병

구문 해설

2행   It may **sound strange**, but they *were* all *made* possible by space research.

- sound + 형용사: ~하게 들리다
- were made: '~되다'라는 의미의 수동태 (← space research made them all possible)

9행   NASA also developed ways [**to *make*** *the signals* {(that are) sent from spacecraft} *clearer*].

- to make: '~하는'의 의미로 ways를 수식하는 형용사적 용법의 to부정사
- make + 목적어 + 형용사: ~을 …하게 하다[만들다]
- sent from spacecraft 앞에는 '주격 관계대명사 + be동사'가 생략되어 있음

Some people say NASA **spends** too much money **on** its space research.

· spend A on B: A를 B에 쓰다

Reading 2   p.74

①

해석

여기 우주 연구에 대한 두 학생의 의견이 있다.

사브리나: 이곳 지구에는 많은 심각한 문제들이 있어요. 그래서 우주 연구에 수십억 달러를 쓰는 것은 말이 안 돼요. 날마다 수천 명의 사람들이 기아로 죽어가요. 어떤 사람들은 우리가 우주로부터 유용한 자원들을 얻을 수 있다고 말해요. 하지만 이곳 지구에도 아직 충분히 사용되지 않는 자원들이 있어요. (우주 연구에 돈을 쓰는) 대신에 태양 에너지와 풍력 에너지에 돈을 쓰는 건 어떨까요?
호세: 가장 중요한 것은 인간이 미래를 위한 계획을 세워야 한다는 것이에요. 오랜 세월이 흐른 뒤 지구는 너무 덥거나 너무 붐벼서 살 수 없게 될지도 몰라요. 그래서 우리는 계속 우주 연구를 이용해서 우주에서 살 만한 다른 장소들을 찾아야 해요. 또한, 호기심은 모든 과학의 시작이에요. 그것이 없었다면 우리는 아직도 동굴에서 살고 있을지도 몰라요! 우리의 호기심은 우리가 놀라운 일들을 하게 도와줘요.

어휘

opinion 똉의견   make sense 말이 되다, 이치에 맞다   die of ~으로 죽다   hunger 똉기아, 굶주림   resource 똉(~s) 자원   yet 분아직   solar 혱태양의   crowded 혱붐비는   curiosity 똉호기심   [문제] safety 똉안전(성)

구문 해설

8행   After many years, Earth may become 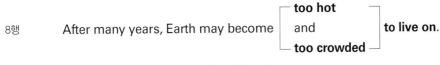 **to live on**.

· too + 형용사 + to-v: 너무 ~하여 …할 수 없다

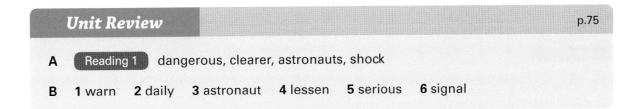

Unit Review   p.75

A Reading 1 dangerous, clearer, astronauts, shock

B **1** warn **2** daily **3** astronaut **4** lessen **5** serious **6** signal

Reading 1   pp.76-77

Before Reading We can use wind energy, solar energy, and hydropower.

1 ① **2** ② **3** (1) ⓐ (2) ⓒ (3) ⓑ **4** ② **5** ③ **6** ②

해석

우리는 살기 위해 에너지가 필요하다. 다행히도, 우리는 어디에서나 그것을 찾을 수 있다! 그것은 햇빛, 물, 그리고 바람 속에 있다. 그것은 심지어 우리 발밑에서도 발견된다!

지구는 에너지, 즉 열로 가득 차 있다. 하지만 그것의 표면은 종종 움직인다. 그래서 열은 종종 그것의 표면을 통해 빠져나간다. 이 열은 지열 에너지라고 불린다. 그것은 지구 표면 근처의 물을 뜨겁게 한다. 이 뜨거워진 물의 일부는 발전소로 옮겨져 증기로 만들어진다. 그 증기는 발전기가 달린 팬을 돌린다. 이제, 우리는 전기를 갖게 된다!

지열 에너지를 사용하는 데는 많은 훌륭한 이유들이 있다. 첫째, 지구는 항상 열을 방출하고 있기 때문에 날씨가 그것에 영향을 주지 않는다. 하지만 풍차는 바람이 필요하고 태양 전지판은 효과적으로 작동하기 위해 맑은 하늘이 필요하다. 두 번째로, 지열 발전소는 작다. 그것들은 다른 발전소들보다 적은 땅을 필요로 한다. 그래서 그것들은 이상적인 장소로 쉽게 옮겨질 수 있다.

지열 에너지는 아직 많이 사용되지 않는다. 하지만, 그것은 우리와 지구에 좋다. 우리 발밑에서 보물을 찾을 수 있다는 것을 기억하라!

어휘

luckily 閠다행스럽게도   sunlight 圄햇빛   be filled with ~로 가득 차다   heat 圄열 (heat up 뜨겁게 하다, 데우다)
surface 圄표면   escape 圐달아나다, 탈출하다; *새어[빠져] 나가다[들어가다]   geothermal 閶지열의   (power) plant
圄발전소   steam 圄증기   fan 圄팬, 선풍기   generator 圄발전기 (generate 圐발생시키다)   electricity 圄전기
release 圐방출하다   windmill 圄풍차   solar panel 태양 전지판   effectively 閠효과적으로   require 圐필요로 하다
ideal 閶이상적인   location 圄장소, 위치   treasure 圄보물   beneath 圀~ 아래[밑]에   [문제] source 圄원천, 근원
danger 圄위험   power 圄동력, 에너지; 전기 *圐동력을 공급하다, 작동시키다   take up 차지하다   fog 圄안개   precious
閶소중한

구문 해설

7행   Some of this heated water ┌─ is brought to a power plant
                              │   and
                              └─ (is) made into steam.

11행   There are many good reasons [**to use** geothermal energy].

• to use: '~하는'의 의미로 many good reasons를 수식하는 형용사적 용법의 to부정사

②

해석

2011년 이후로, 약 680만 명의 사람들이 시리아 내전으로 인해 그들의 집을 떠났다. 이 사람들은 전력을 찾는 데 어려움을 겪고 있다. 하지만 WakaWaka라는 한 회사가 그들에게 작은 태양열 동력 장치를 제공함으로써 돕고 있다.

WakaWaka의 '파워(Power)' 장치는 태양 에너지로 작동한다. 하루 동안의 충전으로, 그것은 150시간 동안 밝은 빛을 제공할 수 있다. 그것은 또한 휴대 전화와 다른 전자 장치에 전력을 공급할 수 있다. 이 장치 덕분에, 사람들은 그들의 친구들과 가족에게 연락할 수 있다. (그러면 그들은 더 많은 사람들에게 그 장치의 훌륭함을 알릴 수 있다.) WakaWaka는 어려움에 처한 시리아인들에게 이미 25,000개의 파워 장치를 제공했다. 이 회사는 또한 '하나를 사면, 하나를 기부합니다'라는 캠페인을 시작했다. 파워 장치 하나가 구매될 때마다, WakaWaka는 또 다른 하나를 기부할 것이다.

어휘

civil war 내전 device ⑲장치, 기구 run ⑧작동하다 charge ⑧청구하다; *충전하다 provide ⑧제공하다 thanks to ~ 덕분에 contact ⑧연락하다 in need 어려움에 처한, 궁핍한 campaign ⑲캠페인 donate ⑧기부하다

구문 해설

2행   These people **have difficulty finding** electricity.
· have difficulty (in) v-ing: ~하는 데 어려움을 겪다

2행   ..., a company [**called** WakaWaka] is helping *by giving* them small solar-powered devices.
· called: a company를 수식하는 과거분사
· by v-ing: ~함으로써

Unit Review p.79

A **Reading 1** heat, escape, electricity, weather   **Reading 2** device

B **1** danger **2** contact **3** device **4** release **5** steam **6** location

Reading 1 해석

사람은 살기 위해 에너지가 필요하다. 그리고 우리는 그것을 지구에서 찾을 수 있다. 지구는 열로 가득 차 있다. 지구의 표면은 움직이고 그것이 빠져나가도록 한다. 우리는 그것을 지열 에너지라고 부른다. 그것은 지구의 표면 근처에 있는 물을 뜨겁게 한다. 우리는 이 물의 일부를 가지고 와서 발전소에서 증기로 바꾼다. 증기는 발전기가 있는 팬을 돌린다. 이것은 전기를 만든다. 지열 에너지는 날씨의 영향을 받지 않는다. 또한, 지열 발전소는 작다. 그래서 그것들은 쉽게 옮겨질 수 있다. 지열 에너지는 지구와 우리에게 좋다.

WakaWaka의 태양열 장치 덕분에, 수천 명의 시리아 가족들은 이제 빛과 전기를 가지고 있다.

UNIT 19 The Arts

Reading 1
pp.80-81

Before Reading I have seen Van Gogh's famous painting, *The Starry Night*.

1 ① **2** has an important cultural value **3** ④ **4** ③ **5** ③ **6** ②

해석

유명한 예술품은 아주 비싸다. 그러나 그것은 또한 중요한 문화적 가치도 가지고 있다. 그래서 그것이 국제 전시회를 위해 박물관에서 박물관으로 이동될 때 사람들은 아주, 아주 주의를 기울여야 한다. 보통 이동을 계획하는 데는 3개월 이상이 걸린다.

그렇다면 예술품을 해외로 보내기 위해 무엇이 행해져야 할까? 먼저, 상자는 포장되기 전에 보통 24시간 동안 박물관에 놓여 있는다. 이것은 상자 안의 공기가 박물관 안의 공기와 확실히 같게 한다. 또한 상자들과 트럭들 그리고 비행기들은 모두 그 예술품을 흔들지 않게 설계된다. 심지어 그것들은 내부에 특수 기후 조절 장치를 갖추고 있다. 이런 식으로, 예술품들은 이동으로 인해 생기는 최소한의 변화를 경험한다. 마지막으로, 보안 경비원들이 있다. 그들은 귀중한 예술품이 도난당하는 것을 막는다. 물론 중요한 예술품들은 보험에도 들어 있어야 한다. 만약 그것이 매우 귀중하다면 보험료는 매우 비쌀 수 있다. (누가 보험료를 지불하는지를 결정하는 것은 쉽지 않다.) '모나리자' 같은 위대한 예술 작품은 수백만 달러의 보험에 들어 있을지도 모른다!

이 모든 것은 매우 어렵게 들린다. 하지만 그것은 우리가 집 근처에 있는 박물관에서 위대한 예술품을 볼 수 있게 해준다.

어휘

artwork 몡예술품   cultural 혱문화의   value 몡가치 (valuable 혱가치 있는)   move 몡동이동(하다)   museum 몡박물관, 미술관   international 혱국제적인   careful 혱조심하는, 주의 깊은 (care 몡조심, 주의)   leave 동떠나다; *~한 상태로 놓아두다   pack 동포장하다   ensure 동반드시 ~하게 하다   be designed to-v ~하도록 제작되다   shake 동흔들다, 진동을 가하다   climate 몡기후   controller 몡조절 장치   work 몡(예술 등의) 작품   experience 동경험하다   lastly 뵘마지막으로   security guard 보안 경비원   priceless 혱매우 귀중한   insure 동보험에 들다 (insurance 몡보험(료))   [문제] thief 몡도둑 (복수형 thieves)   overseas 뵘해외로   least 혱가장 적은 (little의 최상급)

구문 해설

4행   **Usually it takes more than three months to plan** the move.

• it takes + 시간 + to-v: ~하는 데 …의 시간이 걸리다

12행   They **keep the priceless art from being** stolen.

• keep + 목적어 + from v-ing: ~가 …하는 것을 막다

But it **lets us see** great artwork at museums near our homes.

· 사역동사(let) + 목적어 + 동사원형: ∼가 …하게 하다

Reading 2   p.82

⑤

해석

"플래시 사진 촬영은 금지되어 있습니다!" 대부분의 미술관은 방문객들이 사진을 찍을 때 카메라 플래시를 사용하는 것을 원하지 않는다. 왜 그러는 걸까? 카메라 플래시는 그림을 손상시킬 수 있어서이다! 이상하게 들리지만 그것은 사실이다. 카메라 플래시는 열과 빛을 발생시킨다. 열과 빛은 그림이 그려져 있는 캔버스를 훼손시킬 수 있다. 그것은 심지어 물감 자체를 손상시킬 수도 있다. 물론 한 번의 카메라 플래시가 그림을 손상시키지는 못한다. 그러나 미술관들은 수년에 걸쳐 발생할 많은 플래시의 영향에 대해 염려한다. 만일 모든 사람이 플래시 사진 촬영을 한다면 그 영향은 클 것이다. 오랜 시간이 흐른 뒤에는 그것은 마치 그림을 햇볕에 내놓은 것 같을 것이다!

어휘

flash ⑲ 번쩍임, (카메라의) 플래시   photography ⑲ 사진 촬영   allow ⑧ 허용하다   take a picture 사진을 찍다   hurt ⑧ 상하게 하다   light ⑲ 빛   canvas ⑲ 캔버스 천   [문제] display ⑧ 전시[진열]하다   outdoors ⑨ 실외에서   necessary ⑱ 필수적인

구문 해설

4행   They can even damage the paint **itself**.

· itself: the paint를 강조하는 재귀대명사

Unit Review   p.83

A [Reading 1] careful, plan, shake, thieves   [Reading 2] flash

B **1** allow   **2** climate   **3** value   **4** shake   **5** hurt   **6** experience

Reading 1 해석

유명한 예술품은 매우 가치 있다. 그래서 사람들은 그것이 박물관에서 박물관으로 옮겨질 때 주의를 기울여야 한다. 각각의 이동을 계획하는 데는 수개월이 걸린다. 상자 안의 공기는 박물관 안의 공기와 같아야 한다. 또한, 이동 중에 예술품이 너무 많이 흔들리지 않도록 확실히 하는 것이 중요하다. 마지막으로, 예술품을 도둑들로부터 보호하기 위해 보안 경비원들이 필요하다. 또한 예술품은 보험에 들어 있어야 한다. '모나리자' 같은 그림은 수백만 달러의 보험에 들어 있을 수 있다.

Reading 2 해석

시간이 흐름에 따라 그림을 손상시킬 수 있기 때문에 미술관들은 플래시 사진 촬영을 허가하지 않는다.

UNIT 20 *People*

Reading 1   pp.84-85

Before Reading   I think they worked long hours every day. It might have been really hard.

1 ④   **2** ②   **3** hundreds of slaves escape to the north   **4** ④   **5** ③   **6** ③, ④

해석

해리엇 터브먼은 1820년에 미국 메릴랜드 주의 노예로 태어났다. 1849년에 그녀는 성공적으로 도망쳤다. 곧, 그녀는 메릴랜드로 돌아가서 그녀의 가족을 구했다. 그녀는 여러 번 돌아와서 수백 명의 노예들이 북쪽으로 탈출하도록 도와줬다. 그녀의 행동으로 인해, 그녀는 사람들에게 '모세'로 알려지게 되었다.

터브먼이 어린아이였을 때, 그녀는 자기 주인들에게 맞고 채찍질을 당했다. 언젠가 그녀의 주인이 다른 노예에게 무거운 물건 하나를 던졌는데, 그녀가 그것에 대신 맞았다. 그것은 그녀의 머리를 거의 으스러뜨리고 심한 흉터를 남겼다. 그 부상은 여생 동안 터브먼에게 건강상의 문제들을 일으켰다.

노예 소유주들은 터브먼을 잡을 수 있는 누구에게나 돈을 주겠다고 했다. 하지만 그녀는 노예들이 자유가 되도록 계속해서 용감하게 도왔다. 그녀와 그녀가 도와준 어떤 노예들도 결코 잡히지 않았다.

어휘

slave 몡노예   state 몡(미국 등에서) 주(州)   run away 도망치다   beat 동때리다   whip 동채찍질하다   master 몡주인   throw 동던지다   object 몡물건, 물체   nearly 분거의   crush 동으스러[쭈그러]뜨리다   scar 몡흉터   injury 몡부상 (injure 동부상을 입히다)   offer 동제공하다   bravely 분용감하게   continue 동계속하다   [문제] soon after 곧   go through ~을 겪다

구문 해설

3행   She returned many times and **helped hundreds of slaves escape** to the north.

- help + 목적어 + (to) 동사원형: ~가 …하도록 돕다

11행   Slave owners offered money to anyone [**who** could catch Tubman].

- who 이하는 anyone을 수식하는 주격 관계대명사절

12행   **Neither** she **nor** any of the slaves [(that) she helped] were ever caught.
       주어   동사

- neither A nor B: A도 B도 아닌
- she 앞에 목적격 관계대명사 who 또는 that이 생략되어 있음

①

해석

해리엇 터브먼은 미국의 20달러짜리 지폐의 새로운 얼굴이 될 것이다. 터브먼은 100년 만에 미국 지폐 앞면에 나오는 최초의 여성이 될 것이다. 그녀는 미국의 7번째 대통령인 앤드루 잭슨을 대신할 것이다. 노예 소유주였던 잭슨은 지폐 뒷면으로 옮겨질 것이다. (사람들은 그가 평민 남성에게 투표하도록 허가했기 때문에 그를 존경한다.) 새로운 지폐는 곧바로 나오지는 않을 것이다. 사실상, 그것은 2030년쯤 되어서야 나올 것이다. 그럼에도 불구하고, 사람들은 그 변화에 대해 매우 들떠 있다. 그들은 그녀가 가졌던 용기와 평등에 대한 그녀의 신념을 칭찬한다.

어휘

bill 명 지폐   front 명 앞면[앞부분]   replace 동 대신하다, 대체하다   president 명 대통령   respect 명 동 존경(하다)   vote 동 투표하다   appear 동 나타나다; *나오다   admire 동 존경하다, 칭찬하다   courage 명 용기   belief 명 신념, 확신   equality 명 평등

구문 해설

3행   Jackson, [**who** was a slave owner], will be moved to the back of the bill.
· who ... owner는 선행사 Jackson을 부연 설명하는 계속적 용법의 주격 관계대명사절이 문장 중간에 삽입된 형태

Unit Review p.87

A   Reading 1   slave, save, beat, heavy   Reading 2   replace
B   **1** nearly   **2** scar   **3** offer   **4** equality   **5** continue   **6** beat

Reading 1 해석

해리엇 터브먼은 그녀가 1849년에 탈출할 때까지 미국 메릴랜드 주의 노예였다. 그녀는 자신의 가족과 많은 다른 노예들을 구하기 위해 되돌아왔고 사람들에게 '모세'로 알려지게 되었다. 그녀가 어렸을 때, 그녀의 주인들은 그녀를 채찍질하고 때렸다. 어느 날, 그녀는 무거운 물건으로 머리를 맞았다. 이것은 그녀가 평생 동안 건강상의 문제들을 겪게 했다. 노예 소유주들이 터브먼을 잡으려고 애썼지만, 그들은 그녀나 그녀가 도와준 노예들을 결코 잡지 못했다.

Reading 2 해석

해리엇 터브먼은 새로운 미국의 20달러 지폐에서 앤드루 잭슨을 대신할 것인데, 이는 그녀의 용기와 신념에 대한 사람들의 존경 때문이다.

MEMO

MEMO

MEMO

MEMO

MEMO

MEMO

MEMO

JUNIOR
READING EXPERT

Level 1